Cambridge IGCSE® & O Level

Complete

Biology

Workbook

Fourth Edition

Ron Pickering

Great Clarendon Street, Oxford, OX2 6DP, United Kingdom

Oxford University Press is a department of the University of Oxford. It furthers the University's objective of excellence in research, scholarship, and education by publishing worldwide. Oxford is a registered trade mark of Oxford University Press in the UK and in certain other countries

British Library Cataloguing in Publication Data
Data available

978-1-38-200583-8

1 3 5 7 9 10 8 6 4 2

Paper used in the production of this book is a natural, recyclable product made from wood grown in sustainable forests. The manufacturing process conforms to the environmental regulations of the country of origin.

Printed by CPI Group (UK) Ltd, Croydon CR0 4YY

Acknowledgements

®IGCSE is the registered trademark of Cambridge International Examinations.

The publishers would like to thank the following for permissions to use their photographs:

Cover image: Eduardo Rivero/Shutterstock

p16: Jiri Hera/Shutterstock; p110: Kateryna Kon/123RF; p135: Ron Pickering.

All Artwork by: QBS Learning, APTARA, OUP

Although we have made every effort to trace and contact all copyright holders before publication this has not been possible in all cases. If notified, the publisher will rectify any errors or omissions at the earliest opportunity.

Links to third party websites are provided by Oxford in good faith and for information only. Oxford disclaims any responsibility for the materials contained in any third party website referenced in this work.

When using this workbook you will have the opportunity to develop the knowledge and skills that you need to do well in each of the papers in your IGCSE Biology examination.

The IGCSE syllabus explains that you will be tested in three different ways. These are called Assessment Objectives (AO for short). What these AOs mean to you in the examination is explained below:

Assessment Objective	What the syllabus calls these objectives	What this means in the examination
AO1	Knowledge with understanding	Questions which mainly test your recall (and understanding) of what you have learned. About 50% of the marks in the examination are for AO1.
AO2	Handling information and problem-solving	Using what you have learned in unfamiliar situations. These questions often ask you to examine data in tables or graphs, or to carry out calculations. About 30% of the marks are for AO2.
AO3	Experimental skills and investigations	These are tested on the Practical Paper or the Alternative to Practical (20% of the total marks). However, the skills you develop in practising for these papers may well be valuable in handling questions on the theory papers.

Notice that the **recall** questions (AO1) only account for 50% of the marks – you need to show your skill in using these facts for the remaining 50% of the marks.

This workbook contains many exercises to help you to check your recall and to practise these skills. They will be similar to many of the questions you will actually see in your examination, so you will also be helped to develop the skill of working in an examination. In particular, you will find that many of the exercises cover factual material from different parts of the syllabus – exactly like the more difficult questions in the examination.

The answers to the questions are provided, so that you can assess your own performance. Be honest with yourself when checking the marks – you must not be more generous than an examiner would be! Your teacher will probably be able to help you to compare your performance with the expected standards. (Answers to extension questions are not provided.)

Practice may not make perfect, but it will certainly make better.

Good luck!

Ron Pickering

Contents

Contents

1. The seven characteristics of living organisms are **respiration, growth, sensitivity, nutrition, excretion, movement,** and **reproduction**.

   Complete this table by choosing words from this list and writing them opposite their correct meanings.

	Meaning	Characteristic
A	The ability to detect stimuli and make appropriate responses	
B	A set of processes that makes more of the same kind of organism	
C	Removal from an organism of toxic materials, the waste products of metabolism, or substances in excess of requirements	
D	A set of chemical reactions that breaks down nutrients to release energy in living cells	

   [4]

2. To biologists, classification means:

   A giving organisms a name   B identifying organisms

   C putting organisms into groups   D describing organisms

   Underline your answer.   [1]

3. The following is a list of groups that biologists use to classify living organisms.

   class   family   genus   kingdom   order   phylum   species

   Rewrite the list in the correct hierarchy of classification.

   [3]

Extension

4. Write out the complete hierarchical classification for a human.

5. Scientists in South Africa have recently discovered remains of an organism they have named *Homo naledi.* Suggest what this name tells you about the relationship of this organism to a modern day human.

1. The drawings show four common birds that came to feed in an English garden.

Parus caeruleus   *Parus major*   *Turdus merula*   *Erithacus rubecula*

a. State which two birds scientists believe are most closely related and explain your answer.

....

.... [2]

b. i. Complete this table showing the external features of these birds. One example column has been completed.

Species/feature	All feathers the same colour	Dark stripe along length of body	Large pale areas on sides of head
Erithacus rubecula	X		
Parus caeruleus	X		
Parus major	X		
Turdus merula	✓		

[3]

ii. Use the information in this table to complete the following key to identify the four birds.

1. No large pale areas on head   go to 2

   Large pale areas on head   go to 3

2. All feathers the same colour   *Turdus merula*

   Feathers of different colours   *Erithacus rubecula*

   3. ....

   ....

[6]

2. a. Search the internet for images of orang-utan, chimpanzee, ring-tailed lemur, siamang, grass monkey, purple langur, and aye-aye.

   b. Using *only external features* make a key to distinguish between these animals. (Hint: try to begin with a question that divides this group of seven animals into two approximately equal-sized groups.)

   c. These animals are all **primates**. Humans are also primates. Suggest the most important difference between humans and other primates.

   d. Living organisms can also be classified using evidence from DNA. Use the internet to find how much DNA humans have in common with the other seven primates. Suggest which of these animals is most closely related to humans.

1. The diagram shows a single-celled organism called *Euglena gracilis*. This organism has some features which are usually only found in animals and some which are usually found only in plants.

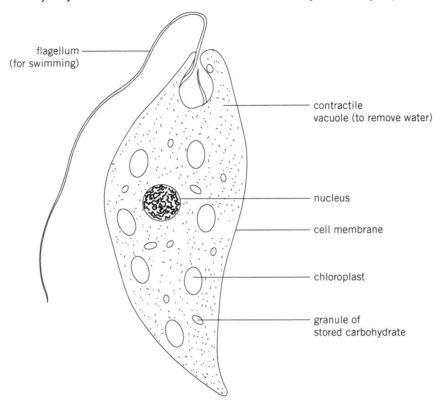

flagellum (for swimming)

contractile vacuole (to remove water)

nucleus

cell membrane

chloroplast

granule of stored carbohydrate

a. i. State **one** feature of *Euglena* which is usually found only in plants.

.... [1]

ii. State the characteristic of living organisms which this structure carries out.

.... [1]

b. i. The contractile vacuole is usually found only in animals. State the characteristic of living organisms carried out by the contractile vacuole.

.... [1]

ii. The flagellum is more often found in animals. State the characteristic of living organisms carried out by the flagellum.

.... [1]

c. All living organisms require a supply of energy. State the name of the process which supplies energy to a cell such as *Euglena*.

.... [1]

Extension

2. Bacteria fit into the classification group called Prokaryotes. The name comes from the Greek language, explain the meaning of this name.

1. **a.** Match up the following parts of a plant with the function performed by each of them.

Part of plant
Stem
Root
Leaves
Flowers
Fruit

Function
Absorb water and mineral ions
Usually help dispersal of seed, a reproductive structure
Hold leaves in the best position
May be attractive to pollinating insects or birds
Trap light energy for photosynthesis

[5]

b. Complete the following paragraphs about the lives of plants. Use words from this list – each word may be used once, more than once, or not at all.

algae   angiosperms   autotrophic   cellulose   chlorophyll
chloroplast   dicotyledons   ferns   herbivorous
monocotyledons   photosynthesis   respiration   starch

All plants contain the light-absorbing pigment called .... This means

that plants are .... – they can make their own food molecules

from simple inorganic sources by the process of .... All the members

of the Plant Kingdom are made of cells surrounded by a cell wall made of ....

The Plant Kingdom includes mosses, ..., and seed plants. Many of the seed plants

have the seed enclosed inside a fruit – they are called ...., and

exist in two groups ....(which have leaves with parallel veins) and

....(leaves have branched veins).   [8]

c. Plants absorb light energy through their leaves.

Suggest how you could calculate the leaf surface area of a tree close to your school.

Extension

1. These four animals were among a group of organisms collected from leaf litter lying on the floor of a deciduous woodland.

ant   earthworm   centipede   mite

a. Complete the table below to compare the four animals.

	Ant	Earthworm	Centipede	Mite
Number of pairs of jointed legs present				
Are antennae present? (**Yes** or **No**)				

[4]

b. Use this key to place each of the animals in its correct group.

1. Jointed legs present	go to question 2
No jointed legs	*Annelid*
2. More than four pairs of legs	go to question 3
Four pairs of legs or fewer	go to question 4
3. Body in two main parts, legs not all alike	*Crustacean*
Body made up of many similar segments, with legs alike one another	*Myriapod*
4. 3 pairs of legs present	*Insect*
4 pairs of legs present	*Arachnid*

Write your answers in the table below.

Animal	Classification group
Ant	
Earthworm	
Centipede	
Mite	

[5]

Extension

c. Insects are members of the phylum *Arthropoda*. Humans have never been able to completely exterminate any insect species, although they have tried to eliminate some species which are pests.

Complete this table to list some species that are harmful and some that are beneficial to humans.

	Name of insect	Reason why it is directly harmful to humans
1		
2		

	Name of insect	Reason why it is beneficial to humans
1		
2		

1. This table compares some features of **chordate** (**vertebrate**) animals.

   a. Define the term chordate (vertebrate).

   .... [1]

   b. Complete this table.

Chordate	Body covering	Constant body temperature	Parental care of young
		No	No
	Moist skin		No
	Scales	No	
	Feathers		Yes
			Yes

   [6]

   c. Humans are vertebrates.

   State how many vertebrae are found in a human backbone. Draw a picture of a single vertebra from the lower back of a human.

   d. State **two** functions of vertebrae.

1. **a.** Many organisms are made up of cells, tissues, and organs.

    Phloem and stamens are examples of structures found in plants.

    State the name of the system to which each of them belongs.

    Phloem ....

    Stamens .... [2]

    b. The diagrams below show a human nerve cell and a palisade cell from a leaf.

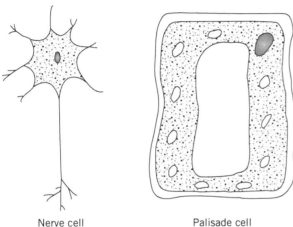

    Nerve cell   Palisade cell

    i. On the diagrams, label **two** features found in both cells. [2]

    ii. State the name of **one** structure found in the palisade cell which allows it to carry out photosynthesis.

    .... [1]

    iii. State the name of **one** other structure found only in plant cells.

    .... [1]

    c. All living cells are able to release energy by the process of respiration.

    i. State the name of the structures in which aerobic respiration takes place.

    .... [1]

    ii. Energy from respiration may be used in protein synthesis.

    State the name of the structures in which protein synthesis takes place.

    .... [1]

Extension

d. i. What is a stem cell?

ii. Where are stem cells found?

iii. Use the internet to find why doctors are very interested in stem cells.

1. The **size** of a structure or organism is measured in units of **length** (such as mm or m). When a diagram is made, or a photograph taken, it may not be easy to directly show the correct size – for example, when a structure is extremely small or very large.

    The correct (or true) size of an organism can be calculated using a combination of actual measurement and a known magnification.

    There are two simple relationships that should be understood:

    $$\text{\textbf{Magnification}} = \frac{\text{measured length}}{\text{actual length}}$$

    $$\text{\textbf{Actual (true) length}} = \frac{\text{measured length}}{\text{magnification}}$$

    It is also important that candidates can use a **scale line** to work out magnification.

    |——————————————————————————|
    5 mm

    > This means that the line drawn represents 5 mm in actual length.

    So, magnification $= \dfrac{\text{measured length of scale line}}{\text{actual length of scale line}}$

    $$= \frac{85}{5} = 17$$

    Note that there are no units for magnification – it is a comparison of lengths. Be careful to make sure that the two lengths you are comparing are given in the same units.

    State

    a. How many mm there are in 1 cm ....

    b. How many μm there are in 1 mm ....

    Core students (Papers 1 and 3) can use millimetres (mm) as units, but candidates taking extension papers (Papers 2 and 4) should also be confident with the use of **micrometres** (μ or μm).

2. The diagram shows a cell from the pancreas of a human. The cell was drawn using a light microscope.

    a. Identify the structures labelled **A**, **B**, and **C**.   [3]

    b. Which of these structures would not be present in a red blood cell?   [1]

    c. Name two additional structures that you would see in a palisade cell from a leaf.   [2]

    d. Use the scale shown alongside the cell to calculate how much it has been magnified. Show your working.   [3]

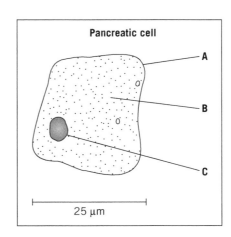

Pancreatic cell

25 μm

1. The diagrams show several types of plant and animal cells. They are not drawn to the same scale.

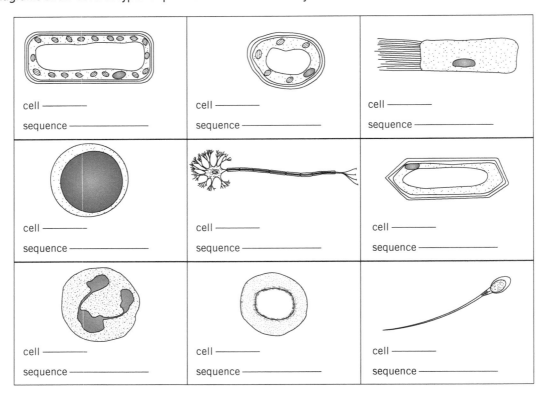

cell —————
sequence ——————

cell —————
sequence ——————

cell —————
sequence ——————

cell —————
sequence ——————

cell —————
sequence ——————

cell —————
sequence ——————

cell —————
sequence ——————

cell —————
sequence ——————

cell —————
sequence ——————

a. Use the key below to identify each of the cells. Write the letter corresponding to each cell on the line next to the appropriate diagram. For each of the cells, write down the sequence of numbers from the key that gave you your answer.

Key

1. Cell has clear and obvious cell wall	go to 2	**5.** Cell has projections at one or more ends go to 6
Cell has membrane but no cell wall	go to 4	Cell does not have projections go to 8
2. Cell has chloroplasts in the cytoplasm	go to 3	**6.** Cell has projections at both ends **CELL E**
Cell does not have chloroplasts in the cytoplasm **CELL A**		Cell with projections or projection at only one end go to 7
3. Cell with fewer than 10 chloroplasts visible	**CELL B**	**7.** Cell has many projections at one end **CELL F**
Cell with more than 10 chloroplasts visible	**CELL C**	Cell has a single long projection at one end **CELL G**
4. Cell contains a nucleus	go to 5	**8.** Cell has nucleus with many lobes **CELL H**
Cell does not have a nucleus	**CELL D**	Cell has a round nucleus **CELL I**

[9]

b. Two of the cells that you have identified would be found in the same plant organ.

State the name of this plant organ. .... [1]

c. A plant body is made of many specialised cells. All of these cells are made by **cell division** at regions called meristems and then **differentiation** of the cells into different tissues. State where plant meristems are found. Suggest how plant breeders could use meristems in producing many copies of useful plants.

Extension

The variety of life crossword

Across:

2 Green pigment found in all true plants
3 Also known as Homo sapiens
4 These invertebrates have jointed limbs and a hard external skeleton
6 The feeding process of all true plants
8 Vertebrates with scales and fins
9 These animals have no backbone
11 An animal group with members that have a backbone
13 A vertebrate with smooth, moist skin
16 A snake is an example of this animal group
17 Five of these groups make up all living organisms
20 The most common animals – includes ants, bees and butterflies
22 A beetle has six of them!
23 All of these arthropods have eight legs
24 These organisms have cell walls but no chlorophyll

Down:

1 Help to keep birds warm
2 The science of putting organisms into groups
5 A type of plant that has leaves that look like needles
7 A method that opens the door for identifying living organisms!
10 A vertebrate with wings and a beak
12 Have fur and feed their babies on milk
14 An organism made up of a single cell
15 A group of organisms that can interbreed and produce fertile offspring
18 A simple plant with no real leaves or roots
19 A simple plant with leaves called fronds
21 Insects have two pairs of these

[24]

11

1. a. Complete these paragraphs about the movement of molecules in and out of cells.
Use words from this list. Each word may be used once, more than once, or not at all.

cellulose	diffusion	down	equilibrium	gas	liquid	osmosis
partially permeable		potential	random	rapid	through	up

.... is a process in which molecules move ....

a concentration gradient. The movement may take place in a .... or a liquid, and

is the result of the .... movement of the molecules. The process continues until an

.... is reached.

.... is the .... of water molecules,

and takes place down a water .... gradient. This process occurs across a

.... membrane.

[9]

b. The table shows the concentrations of two ions inside and outside a cell.

Ion	Relative concentration inside cell	Relative concentration outside cell
K^+	12	150
Na^+	155	6

Match the two columns to show how each substance gets into the cell

Substance
Na^+ ion
K^+ ion
water

Method of movement into cell
diffusion
osmosis
active transport

[2]

Extension

c. The water spider carries a bubble of air underwater. The oxygen in the bubble is used up by the spider and replaced with carbon dioxide, but the spider does not have to come up to the surface to replace the oxygen.

From your knowledge of diffusion suggest why the spider does not have to come to the surface to replace the oxygen in the bubble.

1. A group of students carried out an investigation into the effects of sugar solutions on rods of potato. The rods of potato were cut using a cork borer, then gently blotted and weighed.

   The rods were placed in groups of three in dishes of distilled water or in one of several sugar solutions of different concentrations. After 4 hours the rods were removed from the solutions, gently blotted, and reweighed.

   The students converted the raw results into percentage change in mass for each sugar concentration. The results are shown in the table below.

Concentration of sugar solution / arbitrary units	Percentage change in mass for rod 1	Percentage change in mass for rod 2	Percentage change in mass for rod 3	Mean percentage change in mass
0 (distilled water)	+8	+8	+8	
0.25	+5	+3	+4	
0.5	0	−2	−1	
1.0	−6	−8	−4	
1.5	−9	−10	−11	

   a. i. Calculate the mean percentage change in mass for each of the different solutions. Write your answers in the right-hand column of the table. [1]

      ii. Plot a line graph of the data on the grid to the right. [4]

      iii. From the graph, calculate the concentration of the sugar solution which would result in no change in mass of the potato tuber.

         .... arbitrary units [1]

      iv. Suggest the significance of the value you have obtained for part **iii**.

         ....

         .... [1]

   b. State the name of the process that causes the change in mass of the potato during the course of the investigation.

      .... [1]

Extension

   c. Cooks working in kitchens sometimes soak salad vegetables, especially lettuces, in salt water to remove animals such as small flies, caterpillars, and slugs. However, if the lettuce is left in the salt water for too long the leaves become limp and soggy.

      Explain why the lettuce leaves become limp. Suggest how the lettuce leaves could be made crisp again.

1. The diagram shows different ways in which molecules may move in and out of cells. The dots show the concentration of molecules.

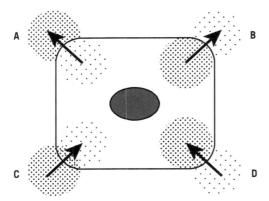

The cell is respiring aerobically.

a. Which arrow represents   i.   the movement of carbon dioxide molecules? .... [1]

                                     ii. the movement of oxygen molecules? .... [1]

b. Which arrow represents the active transport of glucose molecules into the cell? .... [1]

c. Explain your answer to part **b**. ....

....

.... [2]

d. Complete this table to describe **two** other examples of active transport.

Example number	Name of substance transported	Site of transport
1		
2		

[4]

2. Active transport is *specific*. Explain how this specificity is achieved. Suggest how a scientist might develop a drug to prevent the uptake of potentially harmful substances by active transport.

1. Complete these paragraphs about some biological molecules.

    Use words from this list. Each word may be used once, more than once, or not at all.

    **amino acids   cellulose   common   DDT   DNA   fatty acids   glucose   glycerol
    glycogen   haemoglobin   insoluble   simple sugars   soluble   sucrose**

    a. Starch consists of smaller units called .... Another molecule made up of these

        subunits is ...., found in plant cell walls. The sugar most often used for sweetening foods

        is .... which is so useful because it is ....   [4]

    b. Fats are made of smaller units called .... linked to one another by

        .... Fats are often used for energy storage or as barriers between watery environments

        – a property that is useful is that fats are .... in water.   [3]

    c. Proteins such as .... are made of subunits called .... These

        subunits are .... so that they are easily transported from one part of the body to another.   [3]

    d. Nucleic acids such as .... are made of smaller units that act as a code for protein
        synthesis in cells.

        [1]

2. Students are able to test for one essential biological molecule using a solution of DCPIP.

    a. i. Name the biological molecule which can be detected with this test ....   [1]

        ii. State the colour change which shows a positive result for this molecule

            from .... to ....   [1]

    b. The concentration of the essential molecule in a solution can be determined by counting how many drops of the
        solution are needed to bring about this colour change.

        Look at this list of foods.

        milk   orange juice   strong coffee   fizzy drink (cola)

        Suggest which of these foods contains the highest concentration of the essential molecule.

        ....   [1]

Extension

3. Find out which is the most common element in the human body.

4. What proportion of a man is calcium? How much calcium is there in 1 litre of whole milk? How many litres of
    whole milk would be needed to supply all of the calcium in the body of a 70 kg man?

1. Soya is a vegetarian meat substitute made from soya beans.

   The table below gives information about the food values of 100 g of soya and 100 g of lamb.

Food	Energy content / kJ	Fat content / g	Protein content / g	Carbohydrate content / g
Soya	1800	23.5	40.0	12.5
Lamb	1625	21.0	15.0	6.5

   a. i. Use the information in the table to suggest the main advantage of soya compared with lamb.

   .... [1]

   ii. Soya is cheaper to produce than lamb.

   Suggest one reason why soya is cheaper than lamb.

   .... [1]

   b. The nutrient content of different foods can be investigated with a series of simple chemical tests.

   A group of students was given samples of four different powdered foods. They were also given a sample of pure table salt, which only contains sodium chloride.

   They carried out three tests, for glucose, starch, and protein. The table shows the colours produced as a result of their tests.

Food test	Sample W	Sample X	Sample Y	Sample Z	Table salt
Glucose	Red/orange	Blue	Red/orange	Blue	Blue
Starch	Brown	Blue/black	Brown	Brown	Brown
Protein	Purple	Purple	Blue	Purple	Blue

   i. State which one of the samples contained protein but no starch or glucose. .... [1]

   ii. Suggest why table salt was included in the testing. ....

   .... [1]

   iii. Potato contains starch and protein but not glucose. State which food might have been potato.

   .... [1]

Extension

   c. Some popular soft drinks advertise that they contain vitamin C. How could you test a sample of one of these soft drinks to check whether this claim is true? How could you compare the vitamin C content of five different soft drinks?

1. a. Match the following nutrients with their function in the body

Nutrient
calcium
iron
Vitamin C
Vitamin D
phospholipid

Function in humans
A part of the haemoglobin molecule
Required for the absorption of calcium
Forms the main part of cell membranes
Involved in bone and tooth structure
Helps in formation of collagen fibres

[4]

  b. Fruit juice can be an important part of the diet. Many fruit juices contain vitamin C. The concentration of Vitamin C in a solution can be measured by its decolorisation of DCPIP solution.

  i. Some nutritionists believe that storage of fruit juice reduces its vitamin C content. An experiment provided the following results.

Solution	Volume required to decolorise DCPIP / cm³			Mean volume/ cm³
Pure fruit juice	2.20	2.32	2.08	
Stored fruit juice	3.40	3.15	3.35	
Fruit juice heated to 40°C	3.25	3.27	3.23	

Complete the table above by calculating the mean values for the volume of juice needed to decolorise the DCPIP   [3]

ii. State whether heating or storage had the greatest effect on vitamin C content of fruit juice.

.... [1]

iii. Many fruit juices also contain sugar. Explain why drinking large volumes of fruit juice may be harmful.

....

.... [2]

Extension

2. In the 18th century, British sailors were sometimes called 'Limeys'. Explain how they got this name.

1. The table below shows the approximate percentage of water in different parts of the body of a mammal.

Part of the body	Water content (%)
Blood	80
Bone	24
Brain	85
Fat	19
Kidney	80
Liver	68
Skeletal muscle	75
Average for whole body	70

  a. **i.** State which part of the body contains most water per 100 g .... [1]

     ii State which part of the body contains least water per 100 g .... [1]

  b. This table contains a list of some of the properties of water.

Property	Importance to living organisms
Good solvent	
Transparent	
High heat capacity	
High latent heat of evaporation	
Solid ice is less dense than liquid water	

Complete the table to describe **one** way in which each of these properties is important to living things.   [5]

  c. How could you show that the liquid released by breathing out is water?

Results (or observations) are a record of the measurements made during an experiment. There are certain rules about the way these results should be presented. The results should be recorded in a table, like the one shown below:

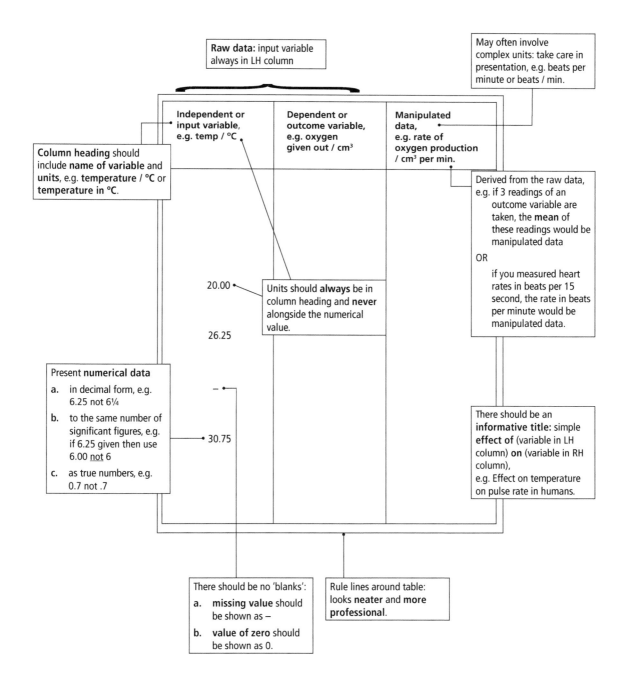

Raw data: input variable always in LH column

May often involve complex units: take care in presentation, e.g. beats per minute or beats / min.

Independent or input variable, e.g. temp / °C

Dependent or outcome variable, e.g. oxygen given out / cm³

Manipulated data, e.g. rate of oxygen production / cm³ per min.

Column heading should include **name of variable** and **units**, e.g. **temperature / °C** or **temperature in °C**.

Derived from the raw data, e.g. if 3 readings of an outcome variable are taken, the **mean** of these readings would be manipulated data

OR

if you measured heart rates in beats per 15 second, the rate in beats per minute would be manipulated data.

20.00

26.25

Units should **always** be in column heading and **never** alongside the numerical value.

Present **numerical data**

a. in decimal form, e.g. 6.25 not 6¼

b. to the same number of significant figures, e.g. if 6.25 given then use 6.00 <u>not</u> 6

c. as true numbers, e.g. 0.7 not .7

–

30.75

There should be an **informative title**: simple **effect of** (variable in LH column) **on** (variable in RH column), e.g. Effect on temperature on pulse rate in humans.

There should be no 'blanks':

a. **missing value** should be shown as –

b. **value of zero** should be shown as 0.

Rule lines around table: looks **neater** and **more professional**.

Sometimes you can see a pattern in your results from the table you have made (see p. 19), but this is not always the case. It often helps to present your results in a different way. **Charts** and **graphs** display your results like pictures and they can make it very easy to see patterns, but only if they are drawn in the correct way. There are rules for drawing graphs and charts, just as there are rules for putting results into tables.

- First of all, look at the variables you measured.

  1. If both of the variables have numbers as their values, you should draw (sometimes we say 'plot') a **line graph**.

  2. If the data can be arranged into groups (sometimes called classes) of equal size then you should draw a histogram

  3. If one of the variables isn't measured in numbers, you should choose a **bar chart**.

- You should always put the **independent variable** on the **horizontal** (*x*) axis and the **dependent variable** on the **vertical** (*y*) axis. If you don't do this, you can easily mix up the patterns between the two variables.

Several topics in IGCSE Biology can easily be tested by asking the candidate to draw a graph. For example, questions on rate of enzyme activity, population change or change in the mass of tissues in different concentrations of a solute.

The basic rules for plotting a line graph are shown opposite.

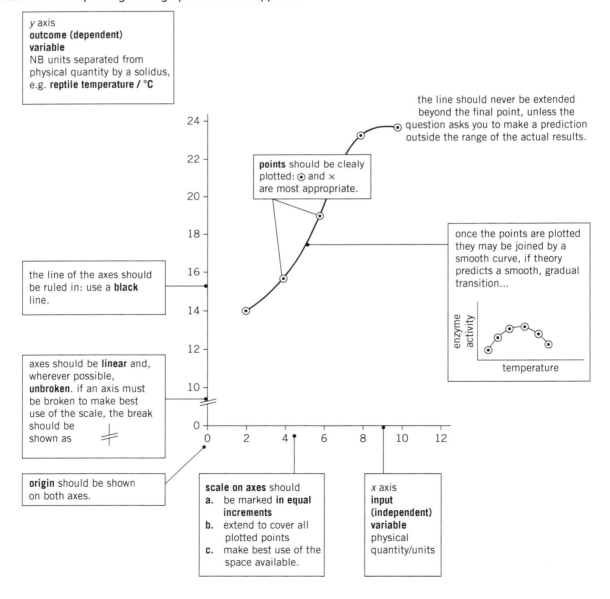

y axis
outcome (dependent) variable
NB units separated from physical quantity by a solidus, e.g. **reptile temperature / °C**

the line should never be extended beyond the final point, unless the question asks you to make a prediction outside the range of the actual results.

points should be clealy plotted: ⊙ and × are most appropriate.

once the points are plotted they may be joined by a smooth curve, if theory predicts a smooth, gradual transition...

the line of the axes should be ruled in: use a **black** line.

axes should be **linear** and, wherever possible, **unbroken**. if an axis must be broken to make best use of the scale, the break should be shown as

origin should be shown on both axes.

scale on axes should
a. be marked **in equal increments**
b. extend to cover all plotted points
c. make best use of the space available.

x axis
input (independent) variable
physical quantity/units

Making predictions

A graph can let you see a pattern between two variables. For example, as protein in their diet increases, so does the weight of mice. The graph can also let you make predictions if it shows an obvious pattern. So, you might be able to predict how much a mouse would weigh if it were fed on a diet containing a certain amount of protein.

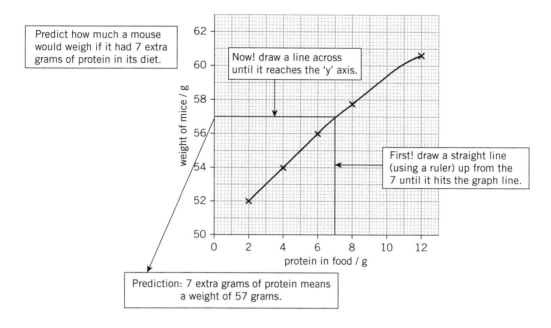

Quantitative or qualitative?

It is often easy to see a simple relationship on a graph, but sometimes not so easy to describe it in the best way.

For example, look at this data below. It was obtained from measurements made on the effect of temperature on the uptake of ions by a plant's roots.

You could be asked to **describe** the results shown in this graph.

A **qualitative** answer would describe this without any numbers. For example, the nitrate absorbed increases up to a peak, then falls away again.

A **quantitative** answer would include numerical information. For example, nitrate uptake increases from 0 to 65 units over a temperature range of 0–35°C. After reaching a peak at 35°C, nitrate uptake rapidly declines to 30 units over the next 10°C.

Which answer provides more information? Which do you think would receive the better mark in an exam?

Of course, many exam questions use the command words describe and explain. If you were asked to do that, you must include some information about the relationship you have described. For example, you might recall that temperature affects the structure of proteins, and that uptake of nitrate depends on active transport which itself depends on protein carriers in root hair cell membranes!

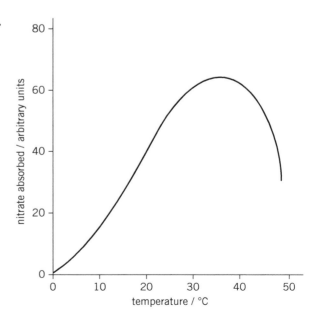

1. The two lists show some words referring to enzymes, and definitions of these words.

   Draw lines to match up the terms with their definitions.

Word
Protein
Substrate
Product
Active site
Denaturation
Optimum

Definition
A molecule that reacts in an enzyme-catalysed reaction
The part of the enzyme where substrate molecules can bind
A change in shape of an enzyme so that its active site cannot bind to the substrate
The ideal value of a factor, such as temperature, for an enzyme to work
The type of molecule that makes up an enzyme
The molecule made in an enzyme-catalysed reaction

[6]

2. This table lists some important uses of enzymes.

Name of enzyme	Use of enzyme
	Part of biological washing powders – removes fatty stains
Restriction enzyme	
Lactase	
	Softens some parts of leather in the clothing industry
	Could break down tough plant cell walls
	Breaks down starch during germination of seeds

   Complete the table by filling in the gaps, using words or phrases from this list.

   amylase   cellulase   **clears pieces of tissue from fruit juices**

   cuts out useful genes from chromosomes   lipase   maltase   pectinase

   protease   **releases carbon dioxide during respiration**   **removes milk sugar from milk**

[6]

Extension

3. Potatoes turn brown when they are cut. This browning may be the result of the action of an enzyme on a substance called catechol. Catechol is colourless, but turns brown when it is exposed to air. Browning makes potatoes less attractive to consumers. How might you prevent cut potatoes from turning brown and unattractive? Do other fruits and vegetables also turn brown for the same reason? How could you tell?

1. Rennin is an enzyme which causes milk to clot. It is used in cheese-making to start making the solid curd.

   A student decided to carry out an experiment on the effect of temperature on the clotting of milk by rennin. She wrote down her results on a scrap of paper.

   <u>Temp and clotting of milk</u>

   60 – nothing   20 – 35 mins. to clot

   30°c – only 8 mins.   40 – fast – 3 minutes!

   15 – nothing again (no clot)

   55 – 7 min

   45 – fastest yet! – 2 min.

                                                      25 – 18 min.

   35°c – 5 minute   50 – 5 min. (same as 35°c!)

   a. Present these results in the form of a suitable table. Draw your table in this space or in your note book.

   [5]

   b. Plot a graph of these results. Use the grid below.

   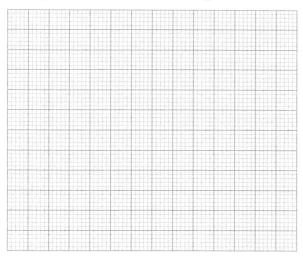

   c. State the optimum temperature for the clotting process ....°C.   [1]

   d. i. State one other factor which could affect the activity of the enzyme.

      .... [1]

      ii. Suggest how a student could control this other factor.

      .... [1]

2. Find out which enzymes are contained in biological washing powders. Suggest how manufacturers could stabilise enzymes so that the temperatures in the washing machines do not denature them.

1. A set of experiments was carried out to investigate the effects of pH on two enzymes, pepsin (a protease) and amylase.

Each reaction was performed at 37 °C and allowed to carry on for 15 minutes. The rate of activity was calculated by measuring the amount of product formed over the time period of the reaction.

The results are shown in the graph (right).

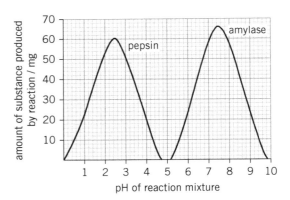

a. i. Name the products produced by the pepsin-controlled reaction.

.... [1]

ii. State how much of this product was formed at pH 2.

.... mg   [1]

b. State the pH at which 60 mg of substance was produced by:

i. amylase ....   ii. pepsin ....   [1]

c. Pepsin works best at low pH (acidic conditions). Explain how these conditions are achieved in the human digestive system.

....

.... [1]

d. Scientists manufacturing Sparklo, a new biological washing powder, were looking for an enzyme which would remove lipids (fats and oils) from clothes.

i. Name the enzyme that would remove fats and oils from the clothing.

.... [1]

ii. Name the products formed as the enzyme digests fats.

.... [1]

iii. Explain how a product of the liver increases the digestion of fats.

Name of liver product .... [1]

Explanation of effects on fat digestion ....

....

.... [2]

2. Think about the conditions found in the human stomach. Suggest why many drugs to be taken orally, such as ibuprofen, are coated in a thin film of waxy material.

1. The rate of activity of amylase is affected by temperature. The effect of temperature was investigated by using a set of six identical test tubes containing 5 cm³ of starch solution. Each test tube was placed in a water bath at a different temperature and then 1 cm³ of amylase solution was added to start the reaction.

   The time taken for the starch to disappear was measured. The results are recorded in this table.

Temperature / °C	20	25	30	35	40	45
Time taken for starch to disappear / s	600	315	210	175	200	420

   a. Use the grid provided to plot a graph of these results.

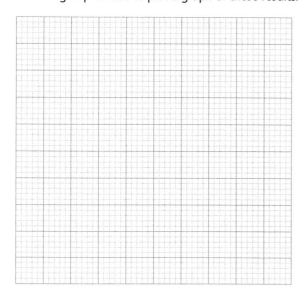

[4]

   b. State the temperature at which the amylase works best.

   ....°C [1]

   c. Explain why it is important that the same volume of starch and amylase was present at the start of the experiment.

   ....

   .... [1]

   d. Chemical reactions usually get faster as temperature increases. Suggest a reason why the rate of amylase activity does not increase above 40 °C.

   ....

   ....

   .... [2]

   e. Name one other factor that would affect the rate of amylase activity.

   .... [1]

1. Complete the following paragraph about plant nutrition.

   The production of food by plants is called .... This process uses

   .... energy trapped by .... in the

   leaves. The process also uses two raw materials from the environment – ....

   from the air and .... from the soil. The first product that can be easily

   detected is .... , a storage carbohydrate. Green plants also produce the

   gas .... during this process – it is released through tiny pores called

   ....   [8]

2. The diagram shows the movement of materials in and out of a leaf during photosynthesis.

   materials in and out of leaf

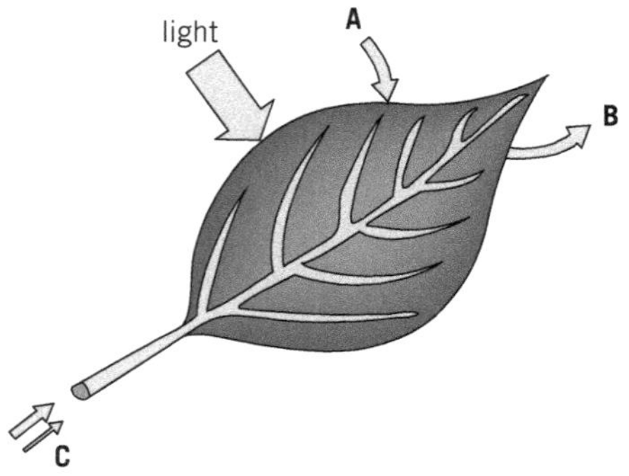

   a. Name the gas entering at **A** ....   [1]

   b. Name the gas entering the atmosphere at **B** ....   [1]

   c. Name the raw material, required for photosynthesis, entering at **C**.

      ....   [1]

   d. Name the mineral, required to manufacture proteins, entering at **C**.

      ....   [1]

   e. State the name of the mineral required for the production of the green pigment in the leaves.

      ....   [1]

   f. It is not easy to measure starch levels in crop plants out in fields. Suggest how a researcher could use a radioactive compound to measure the rate of photosynthesis in crop plants.

1. The diagram below shows a method of measuring the rate of photosynthesis of a water plant such as *Elodea*.

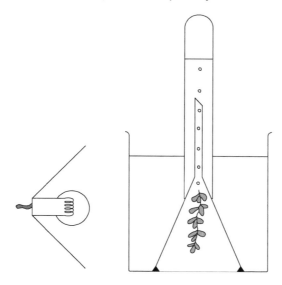

The shoot was exposed to different light intensities and the rate of photosynthesis estimated by counting the number of bubbles released in a fixed amount of time.

The results are shown in this table:

Light intensity / arbitrary units	1	2	3	4	5	6	7	8
Number of bubbles per minute	6	12	19	25	29	31	31	31

a. Suggest the light intensity at which the plant would have produced 22 bubbles per minute.

.... arbitrary units   [1]

b. Explain how the results illustrate the concept of **limiting factors** in photosynthesis.

....

....

.... [2]

c. A common method for measuring the rate of photosynthesis of an aquatic plant is to collect the volume of gas evolved by an illuminated plant. The method assumes that the gas collected has been released during photosynthesis. State the name of this gas. Suggest how you could test that this gas is the one that you predict it is.

1. The diagram shows a section through part of a leaf.

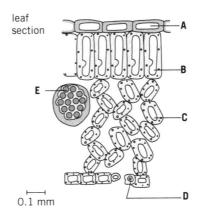

leaf section

0.1 mm

a. Name the cells labelled **A**, **B**, **C**, **D**, and **E**.

Letter	Cell type
A	
B	
C	
D	
E	

[5]

b. State the letter that identifies the cells where most photosynthesis occurs. .... [1]

c. State the letter that identifies the cells which transport water and minerals into the leaf. .... [1]

d. State the name of the carbohydrate that is transported around the plant.

.... [1]

e. Look back at the leaf section. Use the scale to calculate:

   i. the thickness of the leaf

   ii. the length of a palisade cell.

   In each case, show your working. [4]

2. What is meant by the term leaf mosaic? Explain why this is an important term in understanding the efficiency of a plant in photosynthesis.

1. The lower surface of many leaves contains pores called stomata. A single stoma is shown on the diagram below.

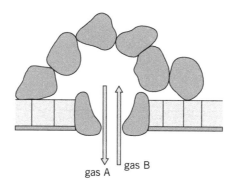

gas A   gas B

a. Gases can move in and out of the leaf through these pores. In the middle of a sunny day **gas A** moves into the leaf and **gas B** moves out.

State the name of   i. gas A ....   ii. gas B .... [2]

b. State the name of the process which moves the gases in and out of the leaf

.... [1]

c. Thistles are weeds which can invade fields of crops. Farmers spray weedkillers onto their fields to try to control thistles. One weedkiller is called **This-stroy**.

A group of scientists decided to investigate the effects of **This-stroy** on the thistles. Thistles were grown in two fields. One field was sprayed with **This-stroy** and the other with water. The thistles were left to grow for 10 days, then collected and their dry mass was measured. The results are shown in this table.

Treatment	Dry	mass	of	weeds	/g	Mean mass/g
This-stroy	20.0	19.1	20.1	19.1	19.2	
Water	33.1	33.3	32.9	32.8	32.9	

i. Calculate the mean mass of the thistles in the two fields. Show your working and write your answers in the table. [2]

ii. Calculate the percentage decrease in the dry mass of thistles when the **This-stroy** is used.

Show your working.

Percentage decrease ....[2]

iii. Suggest why the scientists measured the *dry mass of the thistles*.

....

.... [2]

2. Thistles produce thousands of very light seeds. A Scottish farmer who emigrated to Australia pressed thistle heads in his diary to remind him of home. Twenty years later several Australian states required programmes to eliminate thistles. Explain how this problem might have happened.

1. A group of scientists working in an experimental plant research station were interested in how different factors play a part in the control of photosynthesis. They made a series of measurements under different conditions. Their results are shown in the table below.

	Temperature / °C	Light intensity / arbitrary units	Carbon dioxide concentration / %	Rate of photosynthesis / arbitrary units
A	22	5	0.04	80
B	22	10	0.04	80
C	22	5	0.15	170
D	22	10	0.15	200
E	30	5	0.04	80
F	30	10	0.04	80
G	30	5	0.15	185
H	30	10	0.15	300

a. Describe the set of conditions which gave the highest rate of photosynthesis.

.... [1]

b. The normal concentration of carbon dioxide in the atmosphere is about 0.04%. Use the results in the table to describe the benefits of adding carbon dioxide to the air.

....

.... [2]

c. Explain why the rate of photosynthesis is the same in conditions **A, B, E,** and **F**.

....

.... [2]

Extension

2. Many types of flowers, fruit, and vegetables are available in supermarkets all year round. This is because they can be grown cheaply in some countries and then flown to the area where they will be consumed. Suggest reasons why importing products like this is a good idea, and reasons why it is potentially harmful to the environment.

1. Hydrogencarbonate indicator can be used to show changes in the concentration of carbon dioxide in the air.

CO_2 concentration decreases

CO_2 concentration increases

Purple ←————————————————— Red ————————————————→ Orange/yellow

Celandine is a plant that can survive at low light intensities, such as those found on the ground in a forest. Ox-eye daisy cannot survive in these conditions.

A set of experiments was carried out to investigate the reason for this difference.

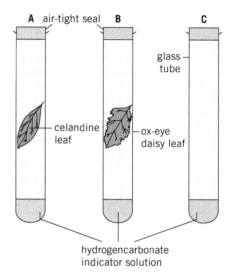

A set of boxes was set up, each lit by a light of a different light intensity. Three glass tubes, as shown in the diagram (right), were placed inside each box. The hydrogencarbonate indicator solution was red in each of the tubes at the start of the experiments.

After one hour the tubes were removed from the boxes, and the colour of the hydrogencarbonate solution was noted. The results are shown in the table below.

Plant	Light intensity / arbitrary units					
species	1	4	8	16	64	128
Celandine	yellow	red	red	purple	purple	purple
Ox-eye daisy	yellow	yellow	yellow	yellow	red	purple

a. Explain why tube **C** is included at each of the light intensities.

....

.... [2]

b. Exactly the same volume of hydrogencarbonate indicator solution was added to each of the three tubes. Explain the reason for this.

.... [1]

c. State which process is occurring most rapidly when the indicator solution:

   i. turns from red to purple .... [1]

   ii. turns from purple to red .... [1]

   iii. turns from red to yellow. .... [1]

d. Suggest why ox-eye daisies do not occur in forest environments.

.... [1]

2. Doctors sometimes advise that houseplants should be provided in hospital wards. Suggest how this could possibly benefit the patients in these wards.

1. The diagrams below show the results of an investigation into the mineral requirements of wheat seedlings.

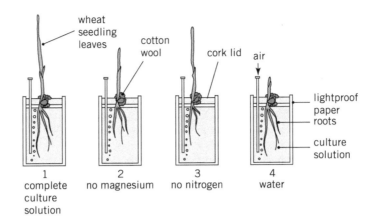

Tube number	Mineral content	Total length of leaves / mm
1	Complete	24.5
2	No magnesium	11.5
3	No nitrogen	20.5
4	No minerals	5.5

a i. Explain why tubes 1 and 4 were included in the investigation.

....

....

.... [2]

ii. Explain why it is necessary to bubble air through the tubes.

....

....

.... [2]

iii. Explain the results for tube number 2.

....

....

.... [2]

b. Farmers often supply these minerals as fertilisers. The bags of fertiliser often have the letters NPK stamped on them.

State what the initials NPK stand for: .... [1]

2. For many years, humans have eaten seaweed as a source of one particular mineral. State which mineral this is, and suggest why is it so important to humans.

IGCSE calculations sometimes involve **percentages**.

What is a percentage?

Percent means 'out of 100'. The % symbol is a quick way to write a fraction with a denominator (bottom line) of 100. For example, instead of saying 'the sun shone 23 days out of every 100', we say 'it was sunny 23% of the time'.

Percentages can be written as **decimals** by moving the decimal point two places to the left:

$$23\% = \frac{23}{100} = 0.23$$

Decimals can be written as **percentages** by moving the decimal point two places to the right:

$$0.45 = \frac{45}{100} = 45\%$$

Formula for calculating percentages

The formulae for calculating percentages or for converting from percentages are shown below.

To convert a fraction or decimal to a percentage, multiply by 100:

$$\frac{1}{4} \times 100 = \frac{100}{4} = 25\%$$

and

$$0.65 \times 100 = 65\%$$

Examples of percentage calculations

The following two examples show how to calculate percentages.

1. Female earwigs have straight pincers. 12 earwigs out of a sample of 25 had straight pincers. Calculate the percentage of females in the sample.

$$\frac{12}{25} \times 100 = 12 \times \frac{100}{25} = 12 \times 4 = 48\%$$

2. A one-year-old snake was 1.5m long. After one more year's growth, the snake had increased in length by 20%. Calculate the length of the two-year-old snake.

$$1.5 \times \frac{20}{100} = 0.3$$

Thus new length = original length + growth = 1.5 + 0.3 = 1.8m

(note that in this example you were given units (m). Don't forget to provide them in your answer).

In any calculation it is important to *show your working*. Even if you make a mistake with your final answer, you will be given credit if you show that used the correct method.

1. a. This pie chart shows the proportion of different food molecules in a diet.

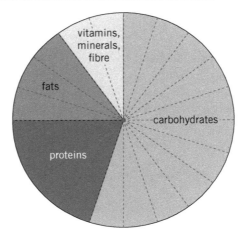

Calculate the percentage of the diet made up of carbohydrates and fats together. Show your working.

[2]

b. Choose whether each of the following statements about food and feeding is TRUE or FALSE.

Statement	True or False
Starch is a carbohydrate found in bread and pasta	
Meat and fish are essential in the diet, as they are the only sources of protein	
Biuret reagent gives a light purple colour with protein	
Oranges and lemons contain vitamin C, and so may help to prevent rickets	
Fats dissolved in alcohol give a milky white colour when mixed with water	
Bacteria can be engineered to provide proteins useful to humans	
Strawberries are a good source of iron	
Vitamin C can be detected using a blue solution called DCPIP	
Assimilation is the process in which foods are transferred from the gut to the blood	
Starch gives an orange colour with iodine solution	
Calcium helps build strong teeth and bones	
Kwashiorkor is a form of malnutrition caused by a low-iron diet	
Too much fat in the diet causes scurvy	
The most common molecule in the human body is water	
Humans cannot eat fungi	

[15]

Extension

c. Protein, a vital part of our diet, is made up of amino acids. How many different amino acids are there? Some of these amino acids are called essential amino acids. What does this mean, and how many are essential for humans? Check why guinea pigs are often used in experiments on human diet.

1. The table below shows the daily energy requirements of different people.

Person	Energy requirement / kJ per day × 1000
Eight-year-old boy or girl	4
Teenage girl	12
Teenage boy	14
Manual worker (builder)	18.5
Patient in hospital	7
Male IT worker	11.5
Female IT worker	9.5
Elderly person (aged 75)	8

a. Plot this information as a bar chart. Use the grid provided.

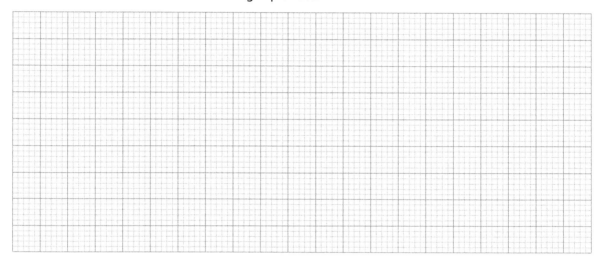

a i. Use data from the table to suggest **two** factors which influence an individual's daily energy requirements.

....

.... [2]

ii. Suggest why a female IT worker might have a lower energy requirement than a male IT worker.

.... [1]

iii. Elderly people often reduce their food intake as they need less energy. Sometimes this reduction in food intake means that they do not take in sufficient quantities of vitamins and minerals.

Suggest the likely problems an elderly person might face if the diet were deficient in:

Vitamin D ....

.... [2]

Iron ....

.... [2]

1. **a.** State the two components of a balanced diet that provide the most energy.

    .... [2]

    b. i. Two students, Jack and Sara, each went to the cafeteria to have a meal.

    The different meals they chose are shown below.

    The total energy content of Sara's meal has been calculated.

    Do you think that the energy content of Jack's meal is greater or less than that of Sara's meal? Write More or Less in the space below the list of Jack's meal.

Sara's meal	Jack's meal
Chicken (150 g)	Burger (120 g)
Jacket potato (150 g)	White bread roll (50 g)
Tomato (40 g)	Tomato ketchup (10 g)
Lettuce (10 g)	Packet of peanuts (50 g)
Cucumber (15 g)	Glass of full cream milk (200 g)
Salad cream (15 g sachet)	
Fruit yoghurt (150 g)	
Total energy content = 2719 kJ	Total energy content ....

    ii. Sara needs about 9000 kJ per day, and Jack needs about 11 000 kJ per day.

    Calculate the percentage of Sara's energy needs that would be supplied by this meal.

    Show your working.

    ....%

    iii. Suggest **three** reasons why Jack and Sara need different amounts of energy per day.

    1. ....

    2. ....

    3. .... [3]

Extension

2. Recent advice given to consumers has suggested that fats in the diet are less dangerous than refined sugars. If the total fat and sugar content supplies all of the energy needs of an individual, why could the sugars be considered more harmful?

If one of the variables in an investigation is not measured in numbers, you should choose a bar chart as a way of presenting the results visually.

This chart displays the results from an experiment in which students were given a choice of one sweet from a selection on a table. Which colour would be their favourite?

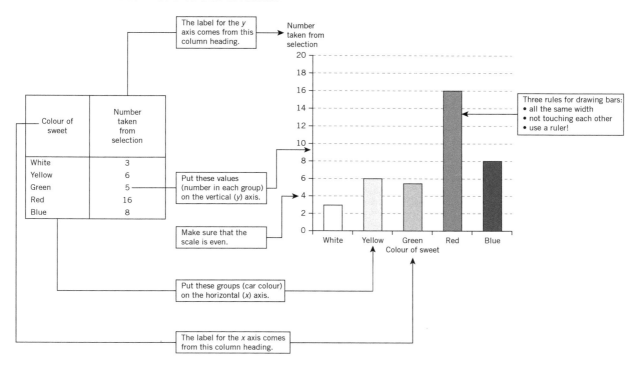

Important: this is a bar chart so the bars do not touch! This is because the data in one bar do not affect the data in the other bars.

1. The table shows the percentage of overweight people in different age groups in a population.

Age group	Percentage of overweight people	
	Male	Female
20–24	22	20
25–29	27	22
30–34	35	27
35–39	40	32
40–44	51	39
45–49	65	44
50–54	64	49
55–59	62	52

a. i. State which sex is more likely to be overweight.

.... [1]

ii. State which group has the smallest percentage of overweight people.

.... [2]

b. i. State the form in which large amounts of extra weight are stored in the human body.

.... [1]

ii. Suggest **three** medical conditions associated with being overweight.

.... [3]

c. Being overweight is one example of malnutrition. Define the term *malnutrition*.

.... [2]

d. A group of doctors studying the growth and development of children noticed that those that did not drink milk often developed weak bones.

i. Name a vitamin present in milk which helps in bone growth. .... [1]

ii. Name a mineral present in milk which helps bone growth. .... [1]

iii. Milk is also a source of protein. Suggest why a shortage of protein may be harmful.

.... [1]

e. Recent reports suggest that the UK, the United States, and Saudi Arabia will have very high levels of obesity within ten years. Suggest why these countries, in particular, might experience such high levels of obesity.

1. Study the two lists below. One is a list of structures in the digestive system and the other is a list of functions of these structures.

   Draw guidelines to link each term with its correct definition.

Structure
Salivary glands
Oesophagus
Stomach
Ileum
Pancreas
Gall bladder
Colon
Rectum

Definition
Produces hydrochloric acid and begins digestion of protein
Produces a set of enzymes which pass into the duodenum
Stores bile produced in the liver
Carries a bolus of food from mouth to stomach
Where most of the water is reabsorbed from the contents of the intestine
Produce an alkaline liquid which lubricates food making it easier to swallow
Stores waste food as faeces
Where most digested food is absorbed

[8]

2. Read this paragraph, which describes what happens to food in the intestines. Use words from this list to fill in the spaces and complete the paragraph. Each word may be used once, more than once, or not at all.

   | bile | bolus | bread | butter | canines | capillaries | carbohydrate | egg |
   | molars | mouth | pancreas | pH | smaller | stomach | surface area |

   An egg sandwich contains starch, fat, and protein. The starch is in the ...., most of the

   fat is in the ...., and much of the protein is in the ....

   When the sandwich enters the .... it is cut into smaller pieces, then crushed by

   the .... This increases the .... so that digestive enzymes can act more

   quickly. The enzymes continue the breakdown of food changing .... molecules such as starch into

   .... soluble molecules. These soluble molecules can pass through the wall of the intestine

   into the ....

   [9]

Extension

3. Many bacteria live in the large intestine. What do they do there? How can humans build up the populations of these bacteria?

1. This diagram shows a section through a molar tooth.

   a. i. Name the parts **A**, **B**, and **C**.

   A ....
   B ....
   C .... [3]

   ii. Name **two** structures found in the pulp cavity.

   1. ....

   2. .... [2]

2. The pH of the saliva of 100 students in a school was measured and compared with the number of teeth which had required fillings.

   The results are presented in this table.

pH of saliva	percentage of pupils in each pH range	average number of fillings per student in each pH range
6.7–6.9	20	8
7.0–7.2	60	5
7.3–7.5	20	3

   a. Suggest how the pH of the saliva could be measured.

   ....
   .... [2]

   b. State the hypothesis being tested in this investigation.

   .... [1]

   c. State and explain whether the results support the hypothesis.

   ....
   ....
   .... [2]

   Extension

   d. How long is a typical human canine tooth? How does this compare with the largest tooth of *Tyrannosaurus rex* or *Carcharodon carcharias*?

1. Human salivary amylase can break down starch. In order to investigate the optimum conditions for starch digestion, four test tubes were set up as shown in the diagram below.

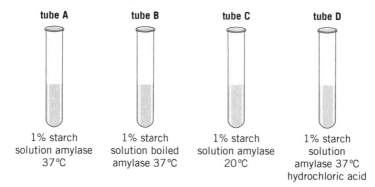

tube A — 1% starch solution amylase 37°C

tube B — 1% starch solution boiled amylase 37°C

tube C — 1% starch solution amylase 20°C

tube D — 1% starch solution amylase 37°C hydrochloric acid

a. After ten minutes, samples were taken from each of the tubes and tested separately with iodine solution and with Benedict's reagent.

Complete the table below to show the likely results of this investigation.

	Colour in tube A	Colour in tube B	Colour in tube C	Colour in tube D
Tested with iodine solution				
Tested with Benedict's reagent				

[4]

b. State where amylase is secreted in the human digestive system.

.... [2]

c. Explain why tubes **A**, **B**, and **C** were incubated at 37 °C.

.... [1]

d. Suggest where the conditions in tube **D** are likely to occur in the human digestive system.

.... [1]

Extension

2. Humans who suffer from cystic fibrosis often have difficulties with digestion of fats and proteins. Suggest why this is the case. What would be the likely effects of this difficulty on the growth of children with cystic fibrosis?

1. Study the structure shown in the diagram (right).

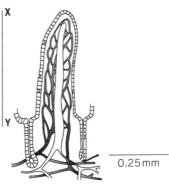

X

Y

0.25 mm

   a. Name this structure. .... [1]

   b. Suggest where this structure would be found.

   .... [1]

   c. i. Draw a line, labelled M, to show the vessel into which fatty acids and glycerol are absorbed.
      [1]

      ii. Draw a line, labelled N, to show a cell which releases a product to protect the lining of this structure.
      [1]

   d. Suggest **three** ways in which this structure is adapted to its function.

      ....

      ....

      ....

      .... [3]

   e. Use the scale line on the diagram to calculate:

      i. the magnification of this diagram

      [2]

      ii. the actual height of the structure, from **X** to **Y**.

      Show your working in each case. [2]

2. Some individuals suffer from a condition called Crohn's disease.

   a. Try to find out the cause of the condition.

   b. Explain why one significant symptom of Crohn's disease is a failure to gain weight during growth.

   c. Suggest how this condition can be treated.

1. These paragraphs refer to transport systems in plants.

   Use words from this list to complete the paragraphs. You may use each word once, more than once, or not at all.

   **active transport   cambium   diffusion   digestion
       epidermis   hairs   ions   magnesium   nitrate
   osmosis   phloem   photosynthesis   respiration   solvent
       support   surface area   transpiration   vascular   xylem**

   Water is obtained by plants from the soil solution. The water enters by the process of ....

   through special structures on the outside of the root called root .... These structures

   increase the .... of the root. As well as absorbing water they can also take up ....

   such as .... which is required for the production of chlorophyll. These substances are absorbed

   both by .... and by .... (a process that requires the supply of energy).

   Plant cells rely on water for ...., as a .... in chemical reactions, and

   as a raw material for .... Water is also used as a transport medium.   [10]

2. One scientist noted that the thistles had a waxy covering to their leaves. He suggested that this waxy coating could help the plants to conserve water

   a. Explain how a waxy coating can help a plant to conserve water.

   ....

   .... [2]

   b. Suggest how a scientist could compare the rate of water loss from a thistle and a crop plant.

   ....

   ....

   ....

   ....

   ....

   ....

   ....

   .... [5]

Extension

3. In parts of the world where flooding of low-lying land is a problem, some crops grow very slowly. Explain why poor drainage causes slow growth in crop plants.

1. Study the diagrams below.

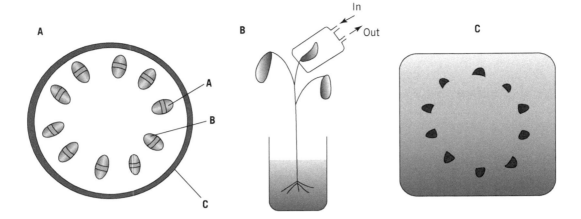

a. Identify the tissues labelled **A**, **B**, and **C** in diagram A.

   A ....   **B** ....   **C** ....   [3]

b. An experiment was carried out using the plant shown in diagram **B**. The roots of the plant were allowed to stand in a solution of eosin (a red dye), and one of the leaves was kept inside a container that could be filled with radioactively labelled carbon dioxide.

   The apparatus was placed in bright light for 6 hours. A cross-section of the stem was then cut using a sharp scalpel.

   i. State which of the tissues **A**, **B**, or **C** would be stained red. .... [1]

      Explain your answer. ....

      .... [1]

   ii. The section was allowed to stand on a piece of film sensitive to radiation.

      When the film was developed it appeared as shown in diagram **C**.

      Explain why the film had this appearance. Use the word 'translocation' in your answer. ....

      ....

      .... [2]

2. Who was the Reverend Stephen Hales? How did he contribute to our knowledge of plant transport systems?

1. The diagram shows the apparatus used by a student in a laboratory investigation of the water balance of a green plant. The roots were carefully washed before the plant was placed in the measuring cylinder.
    The apparatus containing the plant was weighed at the start of the investigation and again 24 hours later. The scale on the measuring cylinder was used to read the volume of water. The same investigation was also carried out by four other students.

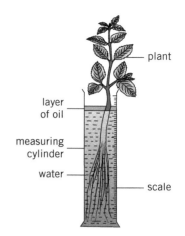

plant

layer of oil

measuring cylinder

water

scale

The results of the investigation are shown in the table.

	Mass of apparatus / g					Mean mass / g	Volume of water / cm³					Mean volume / cm³
Start	220	225	217	221	219		100	100	100	100	100	
24 h later	208	214	209	210	210		87	89	88	87	89	

a. Calculate the mean loss of mass due to water loss from the plant during the 24-hour period.
    Show your working.

    .... [3]

b. Calculate the mean **mass** of water which has been absorbed by the roots of the plant during the 24-hour period.
    Show your working.

    ....g [3]

c. Using your knowledge of how water moves upwards in a green plant, explain why your answers to **a** and **b** are quite similar.

    ....

    ....

    .... [2]

d. Explain why the mass of water absorbed by the roots is not exactly the same as the amount of water lost by the plant.

    ....

    .... [2]

2. Explain why gardeners are advised to water their plants:

    a. in the evening

    b. on the soil rather than on the plant's leaves.

Extension

1. The table lists a series of comparisons between a desert plant and a woodland plant.

	Desert plant	Woodland plant
A	Tissues are more resistant to drought	Tissues are less resistant to drought
B	Leaf system small in comparison to root system	Leaf system large in comparison to root system
C	Stomata often close during daylight	Stomata rarely close during daylight
D	Leaves are often broad and fleshy	Leaves are often thin and rolled
E	Root system has shallow and deep parts	Root system often shallower than desert plant

a. State which of the comparisons is not correct. .... [1]

b. Explain your answer. ....

.... [1]

2. a. The diagram below shows part of a leaf section.

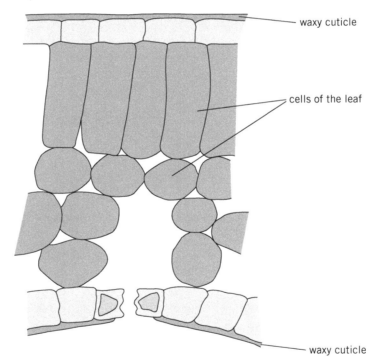

Annotate the diagram to explain how most of the water is lost from the leaf. [3]

b. The leaf was kept at 25°C.

State **two** factors other than temperature which could affect the rate of water loss from the leaf.

....

.... [2]

3. Why do leaves change colour in autumn and winter?

1. The diagram shows a plan of the mammalian blood system.

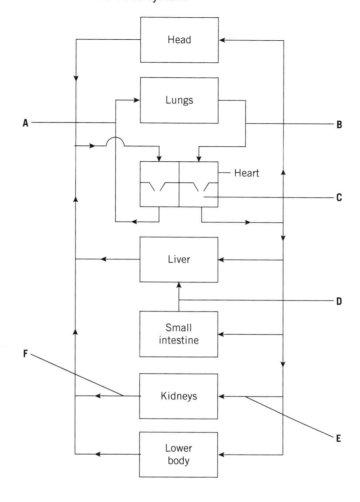

a. i. The name of blood vessel **B** is .... [1]

ii. Suggest **two** ways in which the blood in vessel **A** differs from the blood in vessel **B**.

1. ....

2. .... [2]

b. Suggest **two** ways in which the blood in vessel **E** differs from the blood in vessel **F**.

1. ....

2. .... [2]

c. On the diagram, use a guide line and the letter **P** to show the region where the blood is at its highest pressure. [1]

2. Doctors talk about coronary heart disease (CHD). Why do they use the word 'coronary'?

Standard form is a shorthand way of expressing very large or very small numbers and is used in biology as in the other sciences.

There are rules about showing a number in standard form. We say a number is in standard form when it is written like

$$A \times 10^n$$

Where n must be a whole number, and A must be less than 10.

For example:

$$5.4 \times 10^5$$

Remember that $10^5 = 10 \times 10 \times 10 \times 10 \times 10$ so

$$5.4 \times 10^5 = 5.4 \times 10 \times 10 \times 10 \times 10 \times 10$$

To multiply a number by 10 once, move the decimal point one space to the **right**. In this example we must the decimal point 5 spaces to the right (because we are multiplying by 10 five times). It may help to think of 5.4 like 5.40000.

Doing this, we get

$$5.4 \times 10 \times 10 \times 10 \times 10 \times 10 = 540\ 000$$

In other words, $540\ 000 = 5.4 \times 10^5$ in standard form

Some numbers may be very small, but can still be expressed in standard form.

For example:

$$6.2 \times 10^{-4}$$

This is different because the power is negative, but the principle is the same. Remember that

$$10^{-4} = \frac{1}{10^4}$$

Now, we know $10^4 = 10 \times 10 \times 10 \times 10$.

Having this on the bottom of the fraction means that rather than multiplying by 10 four times, we must *divide* by 10 four times. Dividing by 10 means moving the decimal point to the **left**, so moving it 4 spaces left, we get

$$6.2 \times \frac{1}{10} \times 10 \times 10 \times 10 = 0.00062$$

Therefore, we can see that $6.2 \times 10^{-4} = 0.00062$.

Calculations requiring standard form in IGCSE Biology are most likely to result in large numbers.

For example:

1. A field measures 40 m × 50 m. Students checking the daisy population in the field used 1 m² quadrats, and found a mean value of 37 daisy plants per m².

   Calculate the total number of daisy plants in the field. Give your answer in standard form. Show your working.

Area of field = 40 × 50 m^2 = 2 000 m^2.

Total number of daisies = 37 × 2 000 = 74 000

$$= 7.4 \times 10^4$$

2. There are 5 000 000 red blood cells in each mm^3 of blood.

   a. Write this in standard form .... [1]

   There are 1000 mm^3 in 1 cm^3 and there are 1000 cm^3 in 1 dm^3. Humans have 5 dm^3 of blood.

   b. Calculate how many red blood cells are present in the human circulation. Show your working and show your answer in standard form.

   .... [2]

   c. In a human the red blood cells are replaced approximately every 100 days. Calculate how many red blood cells are produced every day in an average human.

   .... [1]

1. The diagram shows a human heart that has been cut across in the region of the ventricles.

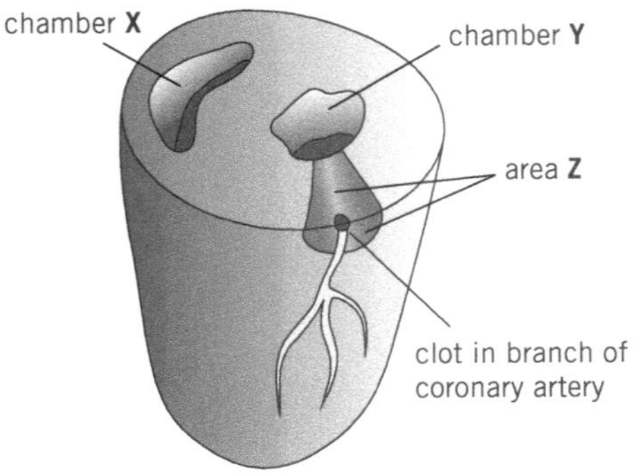

chamber X
chamber Y
area Z
clot in branch of coronary artery

   a. i. State the name of the chamber labelled **Y** .... [1]

   ii. Explain your answer.

   ....

   .... [2]

   b. The beating of the heart is controlled by a patch of tissue called a ....

   In a healthy person the heart normally beats at about .... beats per minute.

2. In mammals, the blood flows through the heart twice for each complete circuit of the body – this is called a

   .... circulation.   [1]

3. In contrast, in fish blood flows through the heart only once for each complete circuit.

   The diagram shows the difference between these two types of circulation.

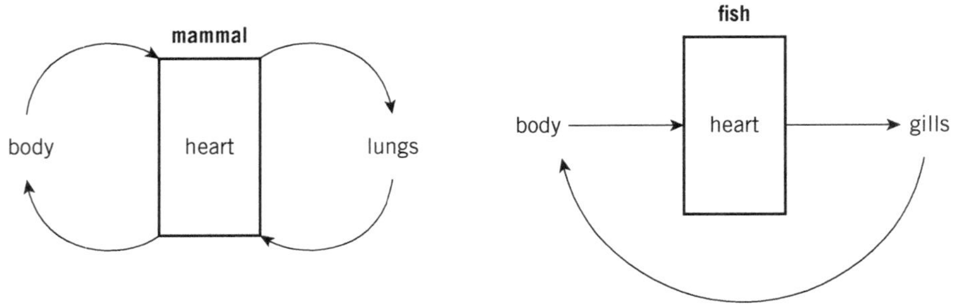

mammal
body
heart
lungs

fish
body
heart
gills

   a. State one **disadvantage** of the single circulation.

   .... [1]

   b. One **advantage** of the double circulation is that pressure is high enough to allow efficient filtration of the blood in the paired .... [1]

   c. The veins of fish tend to be much wider than those of mammals.

   Suggest one reason for this. .... [1]

   d. In a mammal, blood is transported to the lungs in the ....

   .... If pressure in these vessels is too high, ...

   can leak into the lungs. This sometimes happens to climbers at high altitude so the climbers have difficulty in breathing.   [2]

4. Fish have a single circulation, and mammals have a double circulation. What about amphibians?

1. a. The diagram shows the composition of human blood.

    i. Calculate the percentage of plasma in the blood.

    .... [1]

    ii. Name two substances transported in the plasma.

    .... [2]

    iii.Match each of these blood cells with its correct function.

Cell type
Red blood cell
Phagocyte
Lymphocyte
Platelet (cell fragments)

Function
Engulfing invading microbes
Transport of oxygen
Part of clotting process
Antibody production

[4]

  b. The number of red blood cells tends to increase with altitude. Suggest the symptoms that might be experienced by a climber being flown by helicopter directly, without training, to 3000 m.

    ....

    .... [2]

  c. Athletes who compete in races over distances from 1500 to 10 000 m do better if they live or train at altitudes greater than 2500 m. Suggest a reason for their improved performance.

    .... [1]

  d. Some racing cyclists have used the drug EPO to increase the number of red blood cells they have. State the name of one other drug which has been used to 'cheat' in sport. Explain the biological reason for an athlete using this drug.

    Drug ....

    Reason for use .... [2]

Extension

  e. There are 5 000 000 red blood cells in each mm^3 of human blood. The total blood volume for an average human is 5 dm^3. All of the red blood cells are replaced every 120 days.

    Calculate how many red blood cells are produced every day. How many are produced every second?

    Each red blood cell contains about 280 000 000 haemoglobin molecules. Calculate how many haemoglobin molecules must be manufactured every second.

1. The graph shows the pressure changes in the left side of the human heart, during one complete beat.

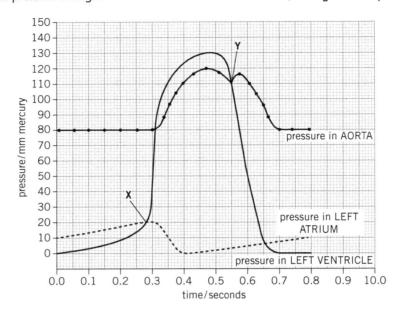

a. Apart from a change in heart rate, how else can an athlete increase the amount of blood pumped per minute?

.... [1]

b. i. From your knowledge of how the heart works, suggest which valves close at points **X** and **Y**. In each case, explain why the valve closes at that point.

[4]

ii. Where else in the circulatory system are valves found?

.... [1]

iii. What is the purpose of these other valves?

.... [1]

c. Suggest why, if the heart is working poorly, a person may have blue lips.

....

.... [2]

Extension

d. One treatment for a failing heart is to have a heart transplant. Following the transplant, the heart may be rejected. Suggest why this happens.

e. A transplant patient may be given immunosuppressive drugs. Explain why such a person may be likely to catch simple infections which another person would not suffer from.

f. Doctors know that there is a shortage of hearts for transplant. They suggest that, in future, people may be given the heart of a pig or a baboon. Suggest why patients may believe that this is not an acceptable procedure.

1. **a.** A group of students carried out an experiment to investigate their pulse rates.

Name	Data collected	Pulse rate / beats per minute
Owen	86 beats per minute	86
Sally	231 beats in 3 minutes	
Ayesha	24 beats in 20 seconds	
Amber	80 beats per minute	80
Stephen	16 beats in 10 seconds	
Ahmed	243 beats in 3 minutes	
Alison	38 beats in 30 seconds	
Manfred	34 beats in 20 seconds	
Kristina	36 beats in 30 seconds	
George	178 beats in 2 minutes	

Their results are shown in this table.

i. Complete the third column of the table. [2]

ii. Describe the pattern you can see in these results. ....

.... [1]

b. The table shows the rate of blood flow in cm^3 per minute to organs of the human body, at rest and during exercise.

Organ	Rate of blood flow / cm^3 per minute	
	Rest	Exercise
Heart	300	400
Muscles	1000	4500
Gut	1500	1000
Kidneys	1100	900
Skin	450	1500
Brain	800	800
Total output	5150	9100

i. State the effect of exercise on the flow of the blood to the organs of the body.

....

.... [3]

ii. Explain why the change in blood flow to the muscles is important.

....

.... [2]

c. Regular exercise reduces the risk of heart disease.

i. Explain why a blockage in the coronary artery can lead to a heart attack.

....

.... [2]

ii. State **two** other factors which increase the risk of heart disease.

....

.... [2]

d. Draw a diagram of the human body to show how a stent is inserted into an artery. Explain why this procedure may be necessary.

1. a. State **one** symptom of a person that has food poisoning.

.... [1]

   b. Describe how a mother could spread food poisoning bacteria to her child.

....

....

.... [3]

   c. Suggest **one** way a mother could make sure that she did not spread bacteria to her child.

.... [1]

2. Not all diseases are spread from person to person. These diseases are **non-transmissible diseases**.

Non-transmissible diseases may be caused by a number of factors.

Suggest **one** disease which may be caused by **each** of the following factors.

Deficiency in diet .... [1]

Inheritance .... [1]

Age-related degeneration .... [1]

Lifestyle .... [1]

Extension

3. What is the Zika virus? Which particular disease is linked to this organism? Suggest how the Zika virus could be controlled.

4. COVID-19 is a disease associated with infection by Coronavirus SARS-Cov-2.

   a. Explain why antibiotics are not used to treat this infection.

   b. Explain how a vaccination programme can lead to protection through herd immunity.

1. **a.** Define the term *pathogen*.

   ....

   .... [2]

   b. Pathogens may be spread in a number of ways.

   Use straight lines to match up pathogens with their methods of transmission.

Pathogen
Cholera bacterium
Influenza virus
Athlete's foot fungus
Plasmodium protoctist
Salmonella bacterium
Human immunodeficiency virus

Method of transmission
By direct contact
In contaminated food
In infected water
In infected body fluids
By an insect vector
In droplets in the air

   [5]

2. This table provides information about some diseases in humans.

   Complete this table.

Disease	Type of pathogen which causes the disease	How disease is spread	One method of control
AIDS	Virus		Antiviral drugs
Athlete's foot		Spores on damp floors in changing rooms	
Cholera	Bacterium		Provision of clean water supplies
Dysentery		In infected faeces	
Food poisoning		Eating infected food	
Influenza		Droplet infection	

   [10]

3. Find examples of diseases caused by pathogens using mosquitoes as a vector. Suggest how humans could try to prevent one of these diseases.

A pie chart (or a circle chart) is a circle, which is divided into slices to illustrate numerical proportion. In a pie chart, the central angle of each slice is proportional to the quantity it represents.

Pie charts help people to see data in a very visual way, although most scientists prefer to use a bar chart to do this. In an exam, you might be asked to complete a pie chart – you would usually be given the outline of a circle with the quadrants drawn in for you.

An example is shown below.

As with graphs, bar charts and histograms, there are certain rules to stick to if you are plotting a pie chart.

- The sectors should be in rank order, with the largest first

- The first sector should begin at 'noon', i.e. at the top of the chart

- Ideally there should not be more than a total of six sectors

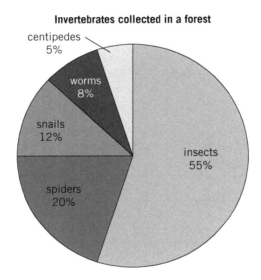

Invertebrates collected in a forest

1. The pie chart shows the number of food poisoning incidents reported from different food sources.

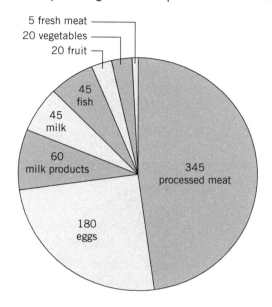

a. Complete this table using the information in the pie chart.

Food source	Number of reported outbreaks
Eggs	180
	45
Fruit	
Milk	
	60
Processed meat	345
	20

[3]

b. Packaging on products such as processed meat usually includes the instruction 'keep refrigerated'.

   Explain why refrigeration makes processed food less likely to cause food poisoning.

   ....

   .... [2]

c. What is the safe temperature in a domestic refrigerator? What is the temperature used to produce pasteurised milk? What about UHT milk?

1. One way in which the community takes responsibility for health is in the provision of a health service. A health service may include screening for disease, and treatment of individuals who are unwell.

About 30% of individuals in Western Europe and the United States will develop some form of cancer during their lifetime.

a. State what is meant by **cancer.** ....

.... [2]

b. The pie chart below shows the percentage of different types of cancer reported in one population of females.

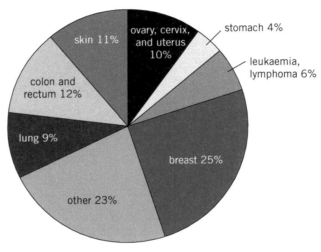

i. State which is the most common cancer suffered by females in this population.

.... [1]

ii. In 2014, one thousand women in this population were reported to have cancer.

Calculate how many you would expect to suffer from lung cancer.
Show your working.

.... [2]

iii. State one type of cancer, shown in this chart, which would not be reported for males.

.... [1]

c. Explain why it is believed that screening for cancer reduces the risk of death from this disease.

....

.... [2]

d. Scientists believe that monoclonal antibodies may be a possible treatment for some forms of cancer. What is a monoclonal antibody, and how might this type of molecule be useful in cancer treatment?

1. Match the following words to their definitions.

Word
Pathogen
Transmissible disease
Antigen
Skin and nasal hairs
Active immunity
Passive immunity
Phagocyte
Lymphocyte

Definition
External barriers to infection
Defence against a pathogen by antibody production in the body
White blood cell that engulfs pathogens
Short-term defence by provision of antibodies from another individual
A disease-causing organism
A substance which triggers the immune response
Cell which produces antibodies
Condition in which the pathogen can be passed from one host to another

[8]

2. This graph shows the level of antibody in the blood in response to two doses of a vaccine.

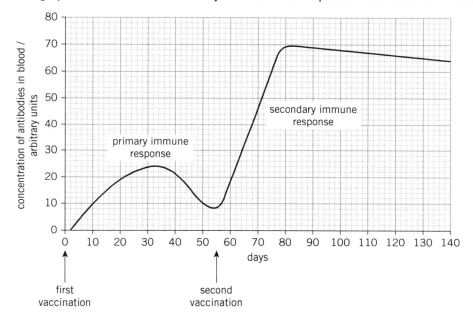

a. Define the term **vaccine**. ....

....

.... [2]

b. State **two** ways in which the response to the second injection is different to the response to the first injection.

....

.... [2]

3. Some human patients are prescribed the drug **warfarin**. What does this drug do? Which dangerous side effect might it have? What was the original use of warfarin?

1. Immunity can safely result from injection of:

   A a pathogen

   B a vaccine

   C an antibiotic

   D blood serum

2. A vaccine has been developed against the organism that causes TB (tuberculosis). The vaccine has been available for use in many parts of Africa since the late 20th century.

   a. Vaccination against TB is an example of **active immunity.**

      Define the term active immunity. ....
      ....
      .... [2]

   b. i. State **three** ways in which **passive immunity** differs from active immunity.

      ....
      ....
      .... [3]

      ii. Complete the table below to show whether each method is active or passive.

Method of gaining immunity	Type of immunity (active or passive)
Vaccination against meningitis	
Antibodies cross the placenta and enter the fetus	
A person bitten by a dog is given a serum	
A baby feeds on colostrum (first milk)	
A person becomes infected with a pathogen	

Extension

3. Type 1 diabetes may be an **autoimmune disease**. What is meant by autoimmunity? Find the name of another important autoimmune disease.

   How can the immune response be harmful to an unborn baby?

1. The diagram below shows an action taken by one group of blood cells against infection by a pathogen.

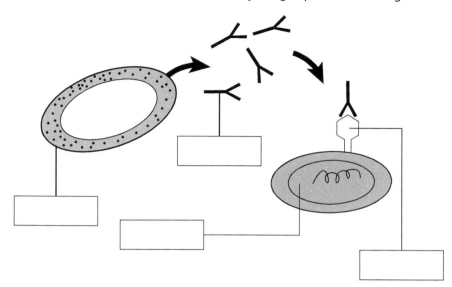

a. Complete the diagram using words from the following list:

   antibody   **antigen**   **antibiotic**   **leucocyte**   **lymphocyte**   **pathogen**

   [4]

b. Suggest **two** ways in which the invading pathogen may be destroyed.

   1. ....

   ....

   2. ....

   .... [2]

c. Doctors can protect the body by providing molecules which stimulate the immune response.

   Name this process of protection .... [1]

2. What is a spike protein? Explain how an understanding of spike proteins is important in protection against viral pathogens.

1. The diagram below shows the large intestine of a human.

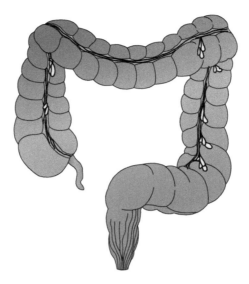

a. Use guidelines and labels to identify:

   i. a region in which water is reabsorbed

   ii. a region in which faeces are stored

   iii. the appendix.   [6]

b. The large intestine may become infected by a bacterium.

   i. Name one disease of the large intestine caused by a bacterium.

   .... [1]

   ii. Describe and explain one symptom of this disease.

   ....

   ....

   .... [2]

c. Explain why a clean water supply helps to prevent the spread of this disease.

   ....

   ....

   .... [2]

Extension

2. Suggest why outbreaks of this disease often occur after heavy rainfall and severe flooding.

1. The diagram shows a section through the thorax (chest).

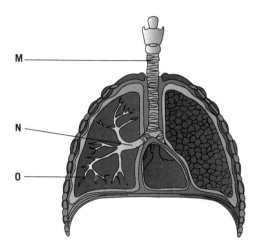

a. Name the structures labelled **M**, **N**, and **O**.

   M ....

   N ....

   O .... [3]

b. On the diagram, use labels and guidelines to identify two different muscles. [4]

c. When muscles contract, they use energy supplied by respiration.

   Give **two** other different ways in which this energy may be used.

   1. ....

   2. .... [2]

d. Exhaled air differs from inhaled air. Name **two** gases which are present in higher concentration in exhaled air.

   .... [2]

Extension

2. Find out whether it is a shortage of oxygen or an increase in carbon dioxide which triggers the breathing reflex. Does a reduction in nitrogen or an increase in carbon monoxide have the same effect?

1. This diagram shows an alveolus (airsac) and a blood capillary.

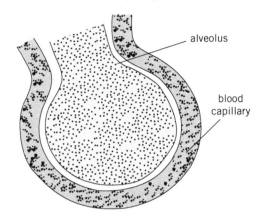

alveolus

blood capillary

   a. On the diagram, use arrows and suitable labels to describe the movement of oxygen and carbon dioxide during gas exchange. [2]

   b. List **three** features which make alveoli adapted to gas exchange.

      1. ....

      2. ....

      3. .... [3]

   c. State the name of the artery that brings deoxygenated blood to the capillary.

      .... [1]

2. a. State the name of one disease which affects gas exchange in humans.

      .... [1]

   b. Explain why this disease reduces the rate of gas exchange.

      .... [2]

3. Gas exchange is necessary for aerobic respiration to occur.

   Write out a word equation for aerobic respiration. [2]

4. What is **pleurisy**? How does it affect human health?

1. The diagram shows the position and shape of the human thorax (chest) during inhalation (breathing in).

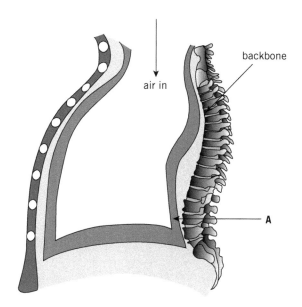

backbone

air in

A

a. State the name of the part labelled **A**.

.... [1]

b. On the diagram label the diaphragm. Use a guideline and the letter **D**.   [1]

c. The diaphragm contains muscles involved in breathing. Name another set of muscles involved in breathing in.

.... [1]

d. Describe and explain the how muscles are involved in exhalation (breathing out).

....

....

....

....

.... [3]

Extension

2. What is the likely vital capacity of a 16-year-old male? Try to find out the vital capacity of Chris Froome, twice winner of the Tour de France.

1. Use the clues below to complete the crossword.

Across:

5 Together with 16 across - a 'packet' of energy - ATP for short
6 A form of energy which may be 'lost'
7 One use of energy which allows organisms to get bigger
9 A method of transport which can move molecules against a concentration gradient
10 Could be defined as 'release of energy from foodstuffs'
12 Organelles in which 10 across occurs most efficiently
13 A chemical process which often requires molecular oxygen
14 Involves replication and separation of chromosomes
15 A change in position of an organism or part of an organism
16 See 5 across
18 The most common substrate for 10 across
19 With 17 down, a metabolic process which joins together amino acids with the use of energy
20 In the absence of oxygen
22 In the presence of oxygen
23 The main source of energy on the Earth
24 The organ in which 10 across can provide the heat to maintain body temperature

Down:

1 Another way of saying 'from the Sun'
2 Muscle...requires a supply of energy
3 Required to carry out the metabolic work in a living organism
4 The most important energy conversion in living things
8 Can be carried out if a supply of energy is available
11 A unit commonly used to describe a quantity of 3 down
17 See 19 across
21 The gas necessary for much of life on Earth – 20% of the atmosphere

2. Cosmonauts return from the Moon with rock samples, and robot space missions bring material from other planets. Scientists suggest that the first sign of life that should be tested for is respiration. Do you agree? Explain your answer.

1. This piece of apparatus is used to study gas exchange.

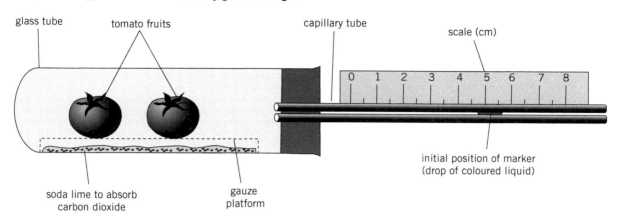

glass tube   tomato fruits   capillary tube   scale (cm)

0 1 2 3 4 5 6 7 8

initial position of marker
(drop of coloured liquid)

soda lime to absorb
carbon dioxide

gauze
platform

a. During the course of the experiment the marker moves.

   i. State the name of the process, carried out by the cells of the tomatoes, which causes this movement.

   .... [1]

   ii. State the direction in which the marker will move. .... [1]

   iii. Explain your answer to part **ii.** ....

   .... [1]

   iv. Calculate the position of the centre of the marker after 40 minutes, if the marker moves 0.25 cm every five
       minutes. Show your working.

                                                                                                                                       [2]

   v. Suggest a suitable control for this experiment.

   ....

   .... [1]

b. The class teacher told the students that fruit growers often enclosed the fruits they collect in plastic bags filled
    with nitrogen gas.

    Explain why this is important.

    ....

    ....

    .... [2]

c. Temperature affects the rate of respiration. Suggest why. How could you check whether your suggestion is a
    valid one?

1. During exercise, muscle contraction requires energy. Some of this energy is released during aerobic respiration.

    a. i. Write a chemical equation for aerobic respiration.

                                                                                [3]

        ii. Suggest why respiration is affected by temperature.

        .... [1]

    b. If the muscles work very hard, the cells may use up all of the available oxygen. When this happens, energy can still be released by anaerobic respiration. These pie charts show the relative amounts of aerobic and anaerobic respiration during a 100 m race and during a 1500 m race.

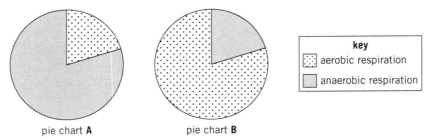

pie chart **A**   pie chart **B**

key
▒ aerobic respiration
□ anaerobic respiration

        i. State and explain which of the pie charts shows the results from a 1500 m race.

        ....
        ....
        .... [2]

        ii. State the effect of a build-up of lactic acid on an athlete's performance.

        ....
        .... [2]

        iii. Explain how the level of lactic acid in the muscles is reduced after a race.

        ....
        ....
        .... [2]

    c. Explain what is meant by an **oxygen debt**.

        ....
        ....
        .... [2]

2. Top athletes can improve their VO$_2$ max. What is this quantity, and why is it so important for endurance athletes?

1. This graph shows the average number of red blood cells of a group of climbers training at different altitudes in the Himalayas.

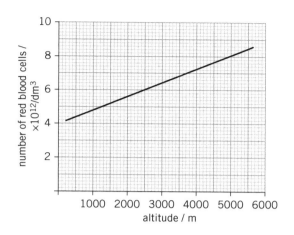

a. State the likely number of red blood cells at 4500 m

.... × 10¹² per dm³ [1]

b. The number of red blood cells tends to increase with altitude.

Suggest the symptoms which might be experienced by a climber being flown by helicopter directly, without training, to 3000 m.

....

.... [2]

c. Athletes who compete in races over distances from 1500 m to 10 000 m do better if they live or train at altitudes greater than 2500 m.

Suggest a reason for their improved performance.

.... [1]

d. People who normally live at sea level have a greater chance of suffering a heart attack if they spend time training at high altitude and rapidly increase the number of red blood cells they have.

Suggest why this is the case

....

.... [2]

Extension

e. Some racing cyclists have used the drug EPO to increase the number of red blood cells they have.

State the name of one other drug which has been used to 'cheat' in sport. Explain the biological reason for an athlete using this drug.

Drug ....

Reason for use .... [2]

1. A group of students wanted to compare the rate of respiration in four different fruits, as well as in tomatoes.

    a. For this experiment, state the **independent variable** and the **dependent variable**, and suggest one variable that should be **fixed**.

Independent variable	Dependent variable	Fixed variable

[3]

    b. This table contains their results.

Tomato	1.55	1.50	1.45	1.50
Damson	0.75	0.75	0.75	0.75
Apple	1.00	1.05	0.95	1.00
Strawberry	1.26	1.20	1.23	1.23
Blackberry	0.90	0.90	0.90	0.90

The students forgot to provide headings for the columns in their table.

Suggest suitable column headings and write them into the spaces at the head of each column.

[4]

    c. Use the grid below to plot a bar chart of their results.

[4]

Extension

2. Fruits to be transported from producer to consumer are often placed in containers with a high concentration of nitrogen gas. Suggest why this is done, and what the benefit might be.

1. a. Define the term **excretion**. ....

   .... [2]

   b. Complete this table about human excretory products.

name of excretory product	site of production	process responsible for product	site of removal of product
carbon dioxide			
		deamination	
sodium chloride		excess in diet	

   [3]

   c. The diagram below shows some of the organs in the abdomen, and the blood vessels which supply them.

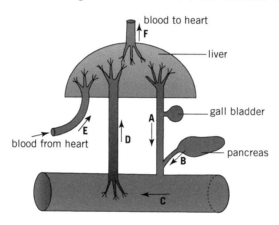

   i. State one important function of the liver. ....

      .... [1]

   ii. Look at the table below. Use guidelines to link each letter with the name of the appropriate structure and a statement about its contents.

letter
A
B
C
D
E
F

structure
hepatic artery
small intestine
bile duct
hepatic portal vein
pancreatic duct
hepatic vein

contents
food
enzymes including amylase and protease
dissolved foods
bile
oxygenated blood
deoxygenated blood

2. A liver transplant may be necessary for some seriously ill patients. Explain:

   a. Why alcoholics may need a liver transplant.

   b. Why even one lobe of a liver can be transplanted to benefit a patient's long-term health.

1. The diagram shows part of the structure of a kidney, and a single cell from region **A**.

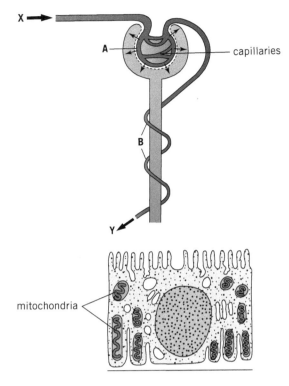

a. Name the vessel supplying blood at **X**. .... [1]

b. Name the ball of capillaries shown in the diagram. .... [1]

c. Explain why glucose can cross the wall at **A** but red blood cells cannot.

   .... [1]

d. Suggest **two** features of the single cell from region **A** which are adaptations to its function.

   1. ....

   2. .... [2]

e. The action of the kidney is to produce urine. Name the tube which carries urine away from the kidney.

   .... [1]

Extension

2. What is a micropipette? Explain how micropipettes have been useful in the study of kidney function.

1. Three test tubes were set up as shown in the diagram below.

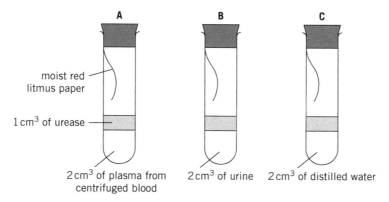

The enzyme urease breaks down urea to release ammonia.

$$urea \longrightarrow carbon\ dioxide + ammonia$$

The tubes were incubated at 37°C for 30 minutes. After 30 minutes the contents of the tubes are subjected to several tests. The results are shown below.

	A	B	C
Test substance			
Biuret reagent	Blue to violet	Remains blue	Remains blue
Benedict's reagent	Blue to orange-red on heating	No change on heating	No change on heating
Moist red litmus paper	Turns blue	Turns blue	No change

a. State the name of the substance that the tests show is present in the plasma and in the urine.

.... [1]

b. Explain why the test tubes were incubated at 37 °C.

....

.... [2]

c. i. Identify which substances are found in blood plasma but not in urine or distilled water.

.... [2]

ii. Explain why these substances are not lost from the body.

....

.... [2]

d. State the function of tube **C**.

.... [1]

2. People who have inefficient kidneys are often recommended to reduce the amount of protein in their diet. Explain why this is helpful. Use simple chemical equations to help your explanation.

1. The diagram below shows a section through human skin in warm conditions.

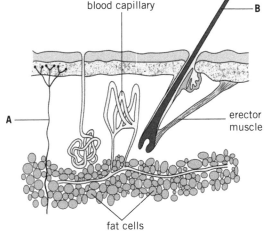

blood capillary

B

A

erector muscle

fat cells

a. State the names of the structures labelled **A** and **B**.

A ....

B .... [2]

b. i. State what happens to **B** if the erector muscle receives a stimulus to contract.

.... [1]

ii. Explain how this response helps to regulate body temperature in a cold environment.

....

....

.... [2]

iii. On the diagram (right) the blood capillary is not complete. Complete the diagram to show the size and position of the capillary in cold conditions.

[2]

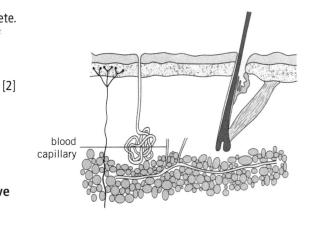

blood capillary

c. The control of body temperature is an example of **negative feedback**. Explain what is meant by the term negative feedback.

....

....

.... [2]

d. One of the symptoms of Type 1 diabetes may be a loss of sensitivity in the feet. Excessive alcohol consumption may damage peripheral nerves and so also reduce sensitivity in the fingertips, toes, and in the small of the back.

Devise a simple test to check for this altered sensitivity. Make sure that you include some form of control in your proposed test.

1. A medical student volunteer agreed to eat a sugary meal then to give a blood sample every hour for the next 12 hours. The blood samples were analysed for the presence of glucose.

The results are presented in this table.

	Time of day /hours	Blood sugar level /mg glucose per 100 cm³ of blood
Meal taken	06.45	80
	07.00	80
	07.30	90
Point **A**	08.00	128
	09.00	120
	10.00	109
	11.00	100
Snack meal taken	12.00	92
	13.00	105
Point **B**	14.00	120
	15.00	94
Point **C**	16.00	100
	17.00	88
	18.00	84
	19.00	92

a. Present these results as a line graph. Use the grid provided.

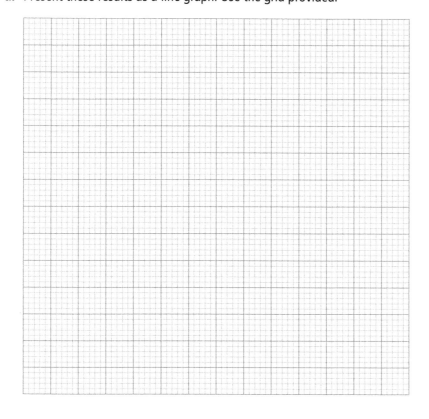

[4]

b. Explain why the blood glucose concentration does not rise immediately after the meal

....

.... [1]

c. **i.** Explain why the blood glucose levels fall at points **A**, **B**, and **C** ....

....

....

.... [2]

ii. Use these results to define the term **negative feedback**.

....

....

....

.... [2]

d. Draw a second line on the graph (use a different colour of pencil or pen) to show the results which might
have been expected for a person with Type 1 Diabetes.   [2]

e. Blood glucose levels increase sharply following a fright or shock.

i. Explain why this happens.

....

....

.... [2]

ii. Suggest **two** other changes which could occur in the functioning of the body because of the fright.

1. ....

....

2. ....

.... [2]

2. How does the drug metformin help sufferers from type II diabetes?

1. This diagram shows a single neurone.

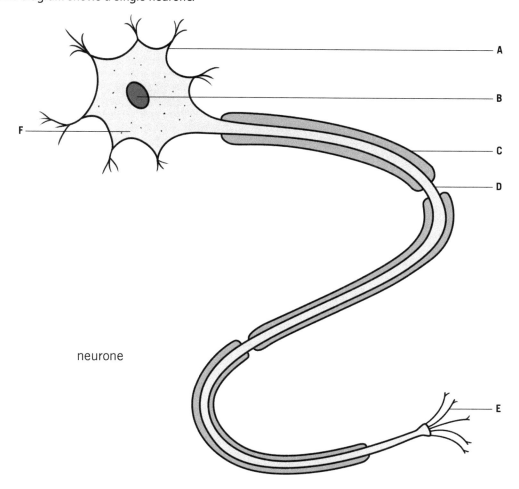

neurone

Match the letters to the descriptions of each of these parts.

Description of part	Letter corresponding to part
Connects with another neurone	
Insulates the neurone to prevent interference with other neurones	
Contains high concentrations of neurotransmitters	
Connects with an effector, such as a muscle	
Allows an impulse to 'jump' quickly along the axon	
Contains DNA	

[5]

2. Serotonin is a neurotransmitter. Find out what it does, and explain why serotonin-specific reuptake inhibitors are important medicines.

1. a. i. Sneezing is a reflex action. Name the organ containing the receptor cells which detect the stimulus that leads to sneezing.

[1]

ii. Suggest **one** advantage of reflex actions.

....

.... [1]

iii. State **two** features of reflex actions.

....

.... [2]

b. i. The diagram below shows a reflex arc.

Select words from this list to name the parts numbered 1–7.

**association neurone   dorsal root   grey matter   motor neurone   receptor
sensory neurone   spinal cord   synapse   ventral root   white matter**

Structure	Name of structure
1	
2	
3	
4	
5	
6	
7	

[7]

ii. Muscles and glands are effector organs. State how muscles and glands react when they are stimulated.

Muscles ....

Glands .... [2]

Extension

c. Are the following statements true or false?

Reflex actions cannot be over-ruled because each of them has a definite survival value.

Some reflex actions have their links in the brain itself.

Reflexes are so important that we don't even know that they have happened.

1. A change in the environment which causes a reaction in a receptor is a:

   A synapse

   B stimulus

   C mutation

   D synthesis

2. The diagram shows a tennis player. The player uses different receptors during a tennis match.

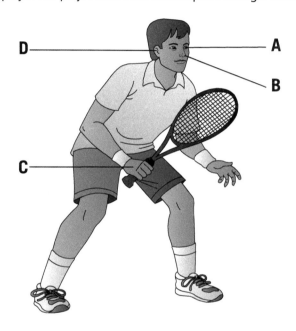

   a. Complete this table to describe the function of these receptors.

Letter	Name of receptor/sense organ	Function of receptor
A		
B	nose	
C		
D		detects position – important in balance

[6]

   b. All receptors convert a stimulus into a 'message'. State the nature of this message, and briefly explain how the messages reach the central nervous system.

   ....

   ....

   .... [2]

3. What is proprioception, and how is it important to humans?

1. The diagram shows a section through the eye.

    a. Use the table below to match up the lettered structures with the descriptions of their functions.

Description	Letter
Contains rods and cones	
Helps to converge light towards the retina	
Is black to prevent internal reflection of light	
Is tough enough to act as an attachment for the muscles that move the eye in its socket	
Is a muscle controlling the amount of light entering the eye	
Contains neurones leading to the visual centre in the brain	

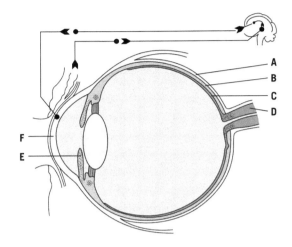

[6]

    b. The diagram also shows the pathway of an important reflex involved in protection of the eye.

        i. Complete and rearrange the boxes to show that you understand the pathway of this action.

receptor is ....

effector is ....   stimulus is ....

response is ....   coordinator is ....

[6]

        ii. State the survival value of this reflex.

.... [1]

2. What are the effects of ageing on the structure of a human eye? Suggest how these effects can be kept to a minimum.

1. a. Define the terms.

    Hormone ....

    .... [1]

    Target organ ....

    .... [1]

    b. State **two** ways in which control by hormones is different from control by the nervous system.

    1. ....

    2. .... [2]

2. Blood glucose levels increase sharply following a fright or shock.

    a. Explain why this happens.

    ....

    ....

    ....

    .... [2]

    b. Suggest **two** other changes which could occur in the functioning of the body because of the fright.

    1. ....

    ....

    2. ....

    .... [2]

Extension

3. Athletes in endurance events are often recommended to consume 'slow release' carbohydrates. What are these, and why are the athletes given this advice?

1. Auxin is a hormone made by the tips of plant shoots.

    a. A shoot was grown in a container so that light shone onto it from one side only. This set of diagrams shows the movement of the auxin in the shoot, and the results of the experiment.

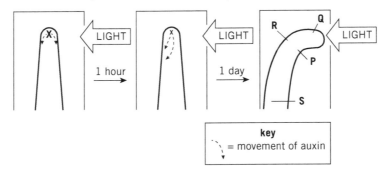

key
= movement of auxin

   i. Describe the movement of auxin in the shoot after one hour.

.... [1]

   ii. Use the diagram to explain how the movement of auxin causes the plant response seen in this investigation.

....

....

....

.... [2]

   iii. Name the plant response seen above, and explain its value to a plant.

       Name of response .... [1]

       Benefit to plant .... [1]

    b. Plant hormones can be used by farmers to manage plant growth.

       Give **two** examples of the commercial value of plant hormones.

       1. ....

       ....

       2. ....

       .... [2]

2. If a rug or sheet of corrugated iron is placed on a vegetated patch of land, the growth of the plants will be affected. Suggest how the appearance of the plants would change if the rug or sheet of metal is left lying on the ground for a month.

1. Choose which of the following sentences is the best definition of the term *drug*.

   A a chemical substance which affects the nervous system

   B a substance which can be obtained from a pharmacy

   C a substance taken into the body that affects chemical reactions in the body

   D a chemical which is useful as a medicine

2. This table shows the prescription of antibiotics for different medical conditions in a clinic

Medical condition	Number of antibiotic prescriptions
Cholera	8
Tuberculosis	22
Chest infection	110
Food poisoning	56
Gonorrhoea	4

   a. Present this information in a suitable fashion. Use the grid below.

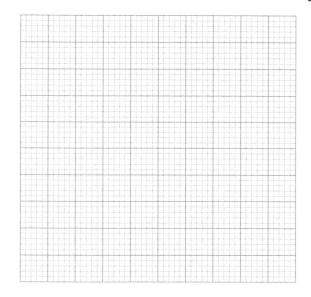

   [5]

   b. i. State which **one** of the conditions treated is a sexually transmitted infection (STI)

   .... [1]

   ii. Calculate the percentage of patients treated for this condition.

   Show your working.

   .... [2]

   c. The doctors at the clinic did not want to prescribe antibiotics for influenza.

   State **two** reasons why they did not do so.

   1. ....

   2. .... [2]

1. a. Study this histogram.

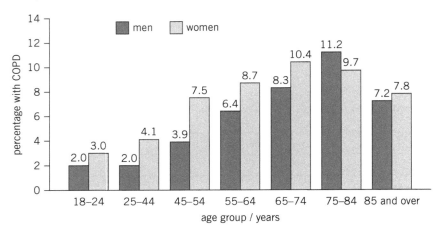

   i. Suggest a suitable title for the chart.

   .... [1]

   ii. State what the initials **COPD** stand for.

   .... [1]

   iii. Does the chart provide evidence that smoking increases the risk of COPD?

   Explain your answer. ....

   ....

   .... [2]

   b. The maximum volume of air that can be exchanged with a single breath in and out is called the vital capacity. A typical healthy male would have a vital capacity of about 5000 cm³.

   Describe and explain the likely effect of long-term smoking on vital capacity.

   ....

   ....

   .... [2]

2. How does nicotine affect the nervous system? Explain how drugs such as nicotine cause physical addiction.

1. Cigarette smoke contains carbon monoxide, which can combine with haemoglobin in red blood cells.

   Explain how you would use your biological knowledge and this additional information to persuade a young woman to stop smoking during pregnancy.

   ....

   ....

   .... [2]

2. This bar chart shows a relationship between smoking and lung cancer.

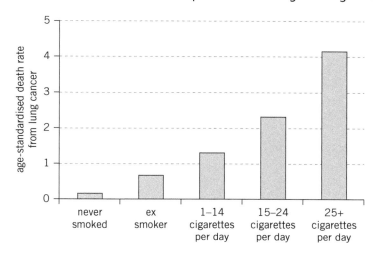

   a. Calculate how much more likely a person who smokes 20 cigarettes per day is to develop lung cancer than a person who has never smoked. Show your working.

   [2]

   b. Some people say that 'just one cigarette a day won't do me any harm'. Use information from the bar chart to help to convince them that this is not the case.

   ....

   ....

   .... [2]

3. The link between smoking and lung disease has been established by **epidemiology**. Explain another link between a disease and a particular lifestyle that has been established using epidemiology.

1. The following information can be found in a standard school biology textbook

   Living organism can pass on their characteristics to the next generation, i.e. they can *reproduce* in two ways:

   Asexual Reproduction

   - involves *only one parent organism*
   - *complete characteristics* of this one parent are passed on to all of the offspring
   - many reproduce asexually *when conditions are favorable (especially when there is much food), and build up their numbers quickly.*

   Sexual Reproduction

   - requires *two organism of the same species,* one male and one female
   - Each individual produces special sex cells or *gametes*
   - Sexual reproduction always involves *fertilisation,* i.e. the *fusion of the gametes.*
   - Offspring therefore receive some *genes from each parent, and thus may show a mixture of the parental characteristics.*

   a. State which type of reproduction

      i. occurs when a bacterium splits into two .... [1]

      ii. is more useful when an organism has to spread quickly through a habitat to which the organism is well adapted

      .... [1]

      iii.leads to greater variation among offspring .... [1]

      iv. involves the process of fertilisation .... [1]

      v. requires the production of cells by meiosis .... [1]

   b. Asexual reproduction can produce a clone of identical plants.

      i. State the meaning of the term **clone**

      ....

      .... [1]

      ii. Explain why the formation of a clone may be a disadvantage

      ....

      .... [1]

Extension

2. What is a hermaphrodite? Name one animal species which is hermaphrodite – what advantage does this give?

1. The diagrams below show simple schemes for asexual and sexual reproduction.

asexual

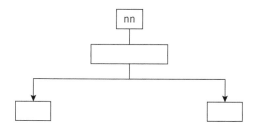

sexual

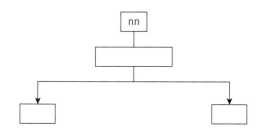

a. Insert the words **meiosis** and **mitosis** in the correct positions on the diagram. [2]

b. Write in the correct chromosome number in the boxes on the diagram. [2]

c. Suggest one **advantage** and one **disadvantage** of asexual reproduction in plants.

   Advantage ....

   Disadvantage .... [2]

d. Explain how both sexual and asexual reproduction could be important in the development of a new crop plant. [2]

Extension

2. a. Define the term 'clone' .... [1]

   b. Scientists have been able to produce clones of laboratory animals such as rats. Suggest how a clone such as this could be useful in the testing of experimental drug treatments.

      ....

      ....

1. Most of the variations in flower structure are related to the methods of pollination.

   a. Define the term **pollination**.

   ....

   .... [1]

   b. This diagram shows a typical wind-pollinated flower.

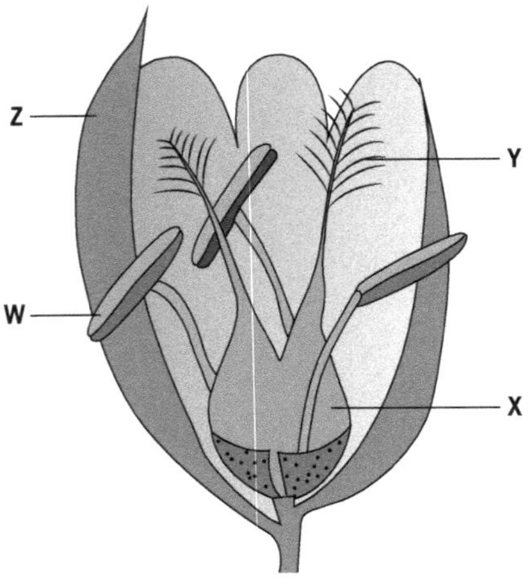

   Identify the structures labelled **W**, **X**, **Y**, and **Z**.

   W ....   **X** ....

   Y ....   **Z** ....   [4]

   c. Complete this table to compare the structure of wind- and insect-pollinated flowers.

Part of flower	Wind-pollinated	Insect-pollinated	Explanation
Petals			
Anthers			
Pollen			
Stigmas			

   [8]

2. Most plants are **hermaphrodite**, but not all are. Explain why **a.** not all holly trees bear holly berries, and **b.** why more than one holly tree must be present in an area for any berries to be formed.

A flower is made up of a set of modified leaves. The leaves are arranged in rings which produce the gametes, protect them, and ensure that fertilisation takes place. The rings of leaves are attached to the end of the flower stalk, the receptacle.

Examination of a typical flower

If a typical flower (a buttercup, for example) is examined, it is possible to see the four rings of specialised leaves. It may be necessary to use a hand lens to do this easily.

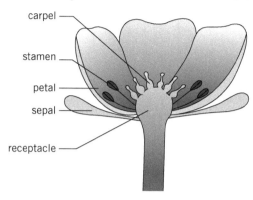

Arrange the four rings (carpel, sepal, stamen, and petal) from outside to inside.

Use a scalpel (take care!) and a pair of forceps to remove a representative part of each ring of leaves. Examine the structure under a hand lens or binocular microscope.

The individual structures will look something like those shown in this diagram.

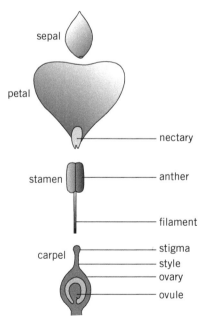

How many of each of the structures can you find in your flower?

Variations in flower structure

Flowers of different species may differ in:

- The number of each of the different components.

- The arrangement of the different parts – especially how fused (stuck together) they are to form tubes or platforms.

Drawing a flower

With so much variation in flower structure, scientists have developed standard ways of describing flower structure. The most common method is to draw a **half flower**.

Use a razor blade or scalpel to cut through the flower, down the line of its stalk. Hold the flower in forceps if necessary, and take care with the sharp blades.

Now draw the flower in section (this gives a three-dimensional view of the petals and sepals).

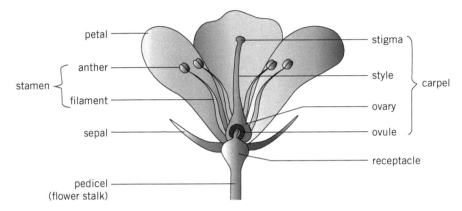

Make sure that the structures are labelled accurately with guide lines drawn with a ruler. (Guide lines always look neater when they are parallel to the top and bottom of the page!)

Add a scale to your drawing.

[6]

1. The diagram below shows a half of a tomato flower.

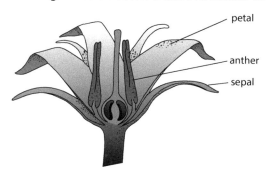

petal

anther

sepal

   a. i. Mark with a **P** the part where a pollen grain must land to pollinate the flower.   [1]

   ii. State the name of the part where the pollen grain has landed.

   .... [1]

   b. This diagram shows a pollen grain with a pollen tube that is growing towards an ovule.

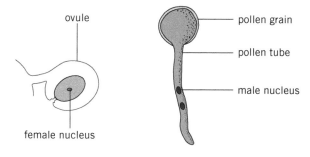

ovule

pollen grain

pollen tube

male nucleus

female nucleus

   i. Complete the drawing of the pollen tube to show how it enters the ovule.   [2]

   ii. Describe and explain what happens to the male and female nucleus at fertilisation.

   ....

   ....

   ....

   ....

   .... [3]

Extension

2. Many fruit growers are anxious about the use of insecticides in areas close to fruit farms.

   Why do some farmers use insecticides? Suggest why the fruit farmers, in particular, are so worried about their overuse.

1. The diagram shows a carpel (the female part of a flower).

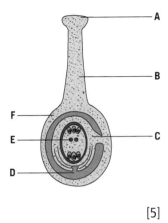

   a. Match the letters on the diagram with the names of structures in this table.

Name of structure	Label letter
Egg cell (female gamete)	
Ovule	
Style	
Stigma	
Micropyle	
Ovary	

[5]

   b. Complete the diagram to show how a male nucleus fertilises the egg cell. Add labels to your diagram. [3]

   c. This diagram shows the appearance of a broad bean seed which has been sectioned and stained with iodine solution.

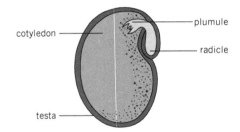

   i. State which parts of the broad bean seed make up the embryo.

   .... [1]

   ii. State the name of the main food material stored in the broad bean seed.

   .... [1]

   iii. Explain what change you would expect to see in the appearance of the seed to make you draw this conclusion.

   .... [1]

2. Many biologists are worried about neonicotinoid pesticides. Explain how overuse of these substances could reduce the production of apples and pears in orchards.

If the data collected from an investigation or experiment can be arranged into groups (sometimes called classes) of equal size, then you should draw a histogram.

A **histogram** shows the frequency of data values on a graph. Like a frequency table, data is grouped in intervals of equal size that do not overlap. A histogram differs from a bar graph in that the vertical columns are drawn with no space in between them (see below). Like a bar graph, the height of each bar depicts the frequency of the data values, as long as the bars are the same width.

Time spent on the computer / minutes	Tally	Frequency
0 – 5	I I I	3
6 – 10	I I I	3
11 – 15	ﬞﬞﬞﬞﬞ	5
16 – 20	ﬞﬞﬞﬞﬞ III	8
21 – 25	ﬞﬞﬞﬞﬞ ﬞﬞﬞﬞﬞ II	12
26 – 30	ﬞﬞﬞﬞﬞ ﬞﬞﬞﬞﬞ IIII	14
31 – 35	ﬞﬞﬞﬞﬞ ﬞﬞﬞﬞﬞ ﬞﬞﬞﬞﬞ	15
36 – 40	ﬞﬞﬞﬞﬞ ﬞﬞﬞﬞﬞ I	11
41 – 45	IIIII	4
46 – 50	IIII	4
51 – 55	III	3
56 – 60	II	2

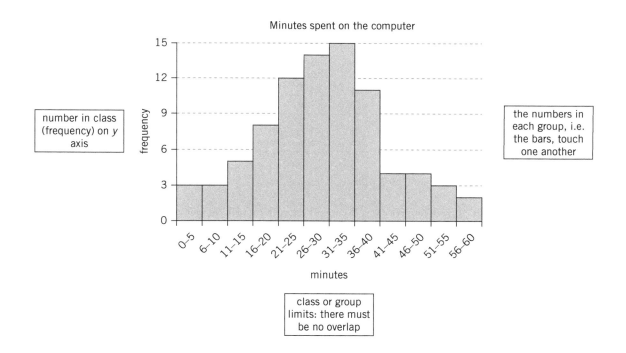

number in class (frequency) on *y* axis

the numbers in each group, i.e. the bars, touch one another

class or group limits: there must be no overlap

1. A broad bean fruit (a pod) contains several seeds. A student opened up 50 broad bean pods and counted the number of seeds in each. He recorded his results in a tally chart.

Number of seeds in pod	4	5	6	7	8
Tally	II	THL THL	IIII IIII IIII IIII II	THL THL THL	I
Total number					

   a. Complete the table to show the number of pods containing each number of seeds.   [1]

   b. Present these results in a suitable graph. Use the grid provided below.

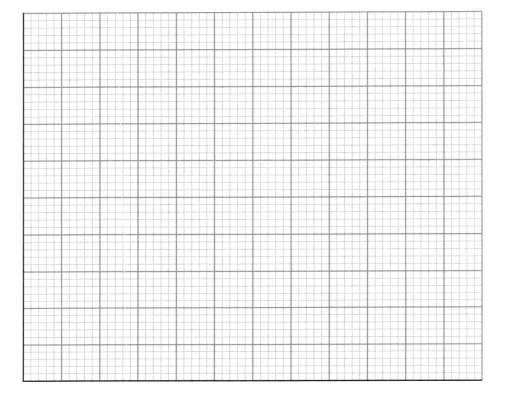

   [4]

   c. State the most frequent number of seeds in a pod. .... [1]

   d. Calculate the percentage of pods which contain the most common number of seeds. Show your working.

....%   [2]

1. Six boiling tubes are available (like those shown in the diagram below). Different items can be added to the boiling tubes so that different conditions would exist in each of them.

The tubes are placed in a bright position.

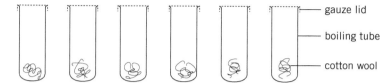

- gauze lid
- boiling tube
- cotton wool

The tubes were set up as shown in the table below, and left for 48 hours.

a. You can add to the drawings of the tubes to show what they might look like at the start of the investigation.

Item/condition	Tube A	Tube B	Tube C	Tube D	Tube E	Tube F
Three pea seeds	✓	✓	✓	✓	✓	X
Black paper cover	✓	X	X	X	X	X
Temperature	warm	warm	warm	cool	warm	warm
Pyrogallol added (removes oxygen)	X	✓	X	X	X	X
Dampness of cotton wool	yes	yes	yes	yes	no	yes
Did seeds germinate?						

Unfortunately you have mixed up your results! Two of the tubes contained germinated seeds, and four did not.

Write **YES** or **NO** in the boxes to complete the table. [6]

b. State the conclusions you can make about the conditions necessary for germination.

....

....

....

....

....

....

....

.... [4]

Extension

2. The action of enzymes in germinating seeds is affected by temperature. Explain why strict control of temperature is important in the malting stage of the brewing industry.

1. This diagram shows the reproductive system of a human male.

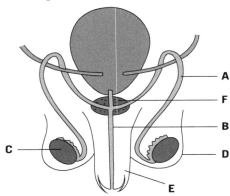

a. State the names of the parts labelled **A**, **B**, **C**, **D**, **E**, and **F**.

   Write your answers in the table below.

A	
B	
C	
D	
E	
F	

[6]

b. Use the letters to state:

   i. the part which produces the male gametes .... [1]

   ii. the part which produces the liquid part of semen .... [1]

   iii. the part which produces testosterone .... [1]

   iv. the part which also carries urine .... [1]

   v. the part which is cut during the process of vasectomy. .... [1]

c. Arrange the following processes into the correct sequence necessary for the production of a human baby.

   A ejaculation   **B** implantation   **C** birth

   D fertilisation   **E** ovulation   **F** development

   ....   [3]

Extension

2. Try to find out what the *Os penis* is. Why is it important? Suggest why it is absent in humans.

1. The diagram below shows a mature human sperm.

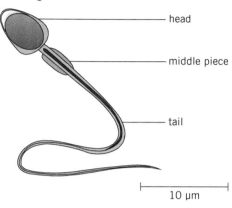

head

middle piece

tail

10 µm

a. The tip of the head of the sperm contains enzymes that break down proteins. State the function of these enzymes during fertilisation.

....

.... [1]

b. The middle piece of the sperm is packed with mitochondria.

Suggest a function for these mitochondria. ....

.... [1]

c. Use the scale provided to calculate the length of the sperm, from the tip of the head to the end of the tail. Show your working.

....   [2]

d. The mass of the nucleus of the sperm is about 3×10^{-6} µg. The nuclei of most other cells in the human body have approximately twice that mass.

Suggest a reason for this difference. ....

.... [1]

e. Female gametes are released at ovulation. The female gamete (ovum) is quite different to the sperm.

Complete this table to compare sperm and ova.

Feature	Sperm cells	Egg cells (ova)
Site of production		
Numbers produced		
Mobility		
Relative size		

[4]

Extension

2. Testosterone is necessary for the development of the male reproductive system. Many older men suffer from an enlarged prostate gland. Suggest the likely symptoms of an enlarged prostate, and explain why testosterone inhibitors may reduce these symptoms.

1. The diagram shows some of the changes associated with puberty.

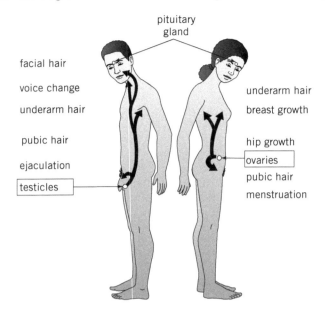

pituitary
gland

facial hair

voice change

underarm hair

pubic hair

ejaculation

testicles

underarm hair

breast growth

hip growth

ovaries

pubic hair

menstruation

a. i. Name the gland which first provides the signals to begin the changes associated with puberty.

.... [1]

   ii. Name the hormone responsible for these changes in a male.

.... [1]

b. Suggest why the breasts grow bigger and the hips grow wider as a female passes puberty.

Breasts ....

Hips .... [2]

c. Menstruation is a sign of the monthly menstrual cycles.

State the name of the end of active menstrual cycles in the female.

.... [1]

Extension

2. Menstruation may be delayed by extreme physical activity. Suggest how this might happen, and how this may cause problems for young women.

1. a. The calendar below shows the menstrual cycle for a woman in June 2020.

Monday	Tuesday	Wednesday	Thursday	Friday	Saturday	Sunday
		1	2	3	4	5
6	7	8	9	10	11	12
13	14	15	16	17	18	19
20	21	22	23	24	25	26
27	28	29	30			

key: ⊠ = ovulation (the release of an egg) ▨ = menstruation ▥ = when the egg is in the oviduct

i. State how many days of menstruation are shown during June 2020.

.... [1]

ii. Assume that this woman has identical menstrual cycles from month to month. State the date in early July 2020 that would be the last day of menstruation.

.... [1]

iii. Explain why fertilisation could not occur on the 7th June 2020 even if active sperms are released into the vagina.

.... [1]

b. The changes in the thickness of the uterus wall during the menstrual cycle are affected by the hormones progesterone and oestrogen.

i. State which hormone reaches its maximum 1 to 2 days before menstruation.

.... [1]

ii. State which hormone reaches its maximum 1 to 2 days before ovulation.

.... [1]

c. The hormone oestrogen is also involved in the changes to the female's body that occur at puberty.

i. State the name of the equivalent male hormone that influences the male body at puberty.

.... [1]

ii. List **three** changes that occur in the male body at puberty.

....

....

.... [3]

Extension

1. The diagram below shows a front view of the human female reproductive system.

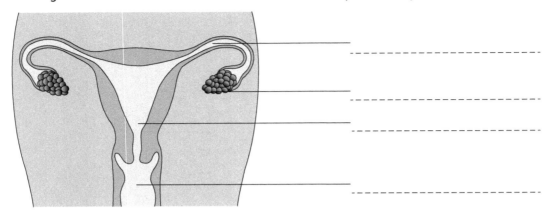

    ----

    a. Add labels to the diagram.   [4]

    b. i. Place a letter F on the diagram to show where the sperm usually fertilises the egg.   [1]

       ii. State the name of the structure formed when an egg is fertilised.

    .... [1]

    c. Match each of the following terms with the appropriate definition.

    AID   conception   copulation   development   fertilisation   implantation

Definition	Term
The fusion of male and female gametes	
The beginning of development of a new individual	
Sexual intercourse	
Fertilisation using sperm from a donor male	
The attachment of the fertilised egg to the lining of the uterus	
The stages which occur as cells divide and become organised into tissues and organs	

[5]

Extension

2. A woman gave birth to triplets, two identical sons and a daughter. Describe the events that occurred at the time of fertilisation or shortly afterwards to result in this multiple birth.

3. Remind yourself of the definition of fertilisation. Suggest how a female gamete prevents 'fertilisation' by more than one male gamete.

1. a. State two reasons for using a condom during sexual intercourse.

   ....

   .... [2]

   b. A student researching methods of contraception found the rates of failure listed in the table below.

Method	Rate of failure	Ranking
Condom	1 in 7	
Coil or IUD	1 in 20	
Diaphragm	1 in 8	
Pill	1 in 300	
Rhythm	1 in 4	
Sterilisation	1 in 30 000	

   i. Complete the rank order in the table. The best method, i.e. lowest rate of failure, scores 1 and the one with the greatest rate of failure scores 6. [1]

   ii. Explain how the contraceptive pill prevents pregnancy.

   ....

   ....

   ....

   .... [3]

   iii. If 1000 women were using the IUD calculate how many would become pregnant after one year. Show your working.

   .... [2]

2. It is now possible in some countries to receive 'morning after' contraception. Suggest one advantage and one disadvantage of this.

1. The diagram below shows a human uterus containing a developing fetus.

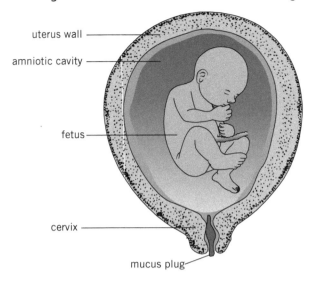

uterus wall

amniotic cavity

fetus

cervix

mucus plug

a. i. Name two structures shown in the diagram which protect the fetus.

   For each structure you have named, explain how it carries out its protective function.

   Structure 1: name .... [1]

   Explanation of function ....

   .... [1]

   Structure 2: name .... [1]

   Explanation of function ....

   .... [1]

   ii. Draw in the position of the placenta on this diagram.   [1]

b. Complete this table by placing a tick (✓) in ONE box on each line to show the movement, if any, of each substance across the placenta.

Substance	From mother to fetus	From fetus to mother	No movement across placenta
Glucose			
Haemoglobin			
Nicotine			
Amino acids			
Carbon dioxide			
Alcohol			
Urea			

[7]

2. Humans are placental mammals. What are monotremes and marsupials? Explain how they differ from placental mammals.

1. At the end of the period of development, a sequence of events leads to the birth of the baby. The final stage is called labour, and begins with the contraction of the uterus muscle.

   Complete this paragraph to describe which hormones are involved in controlling this process.

   Choose words from the following list. Words may be used once, more than once, or not at all.

   adrenaline   falls   oestrogen   oxytocin   progesterone   rises   testosterone

   The contractions of the uterus are prevented by ...., and the concentration of this hormone .... as birth approaches.

   The contractions are stimulated by ...., a hormone which also stimulates lactation.

   The contractions are helped by ...., so the level of this hormone .... as birth approaches.

2. **a.** A baby is about to be born after a full-term pregnancy.

   i. State the name of the period between implantation of the zygote and birth.

   .... [1]

   ii. Suggest how long this period is in most women. Choose your answer from the following alternatives.

   one month   42 weeks   one year   38 weeks   [1]

   b. i. Suggest why it is better for the baby to be born head first.

   ....

   .... [1]

   ii. State how the baby is pushed out of the uterus at birth.

   ....

   .... [1]

Extension

3. Suggest why breastfeeding can act as a natural method of contraception.

1. Gonorrhoea is a sexually transmitted infection (an STI).

   a. i. State which **type** of organism causes gonorrhoea.

   .... [1]

   ii. State **one** early symptom of gonorrhoea.

   .... [1]

   iii. State which method of contraception is most likely to prevent transmission of this disease.

   .... [1]

   b. The bar chart below shows the number of new cases of gonorrhoea treated in the United Kingdom from 2011 to 2016. The numbers of males and females treated are shown separately.

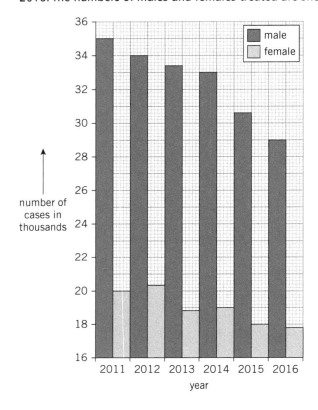

   i. State in which year the largest number of new cases of gonorrhoea was treated.

   .... [1]

   ii. State in which year there was the greatest difference between the number of new males treated and the number of new females treated.

   .... [1]

   iii. Calculate the proportion of the total new cases in 2015 which were for the treatment of females. Show your working.

   [3]

   c. Another STI is AIDS.

   i. Explain how AIDS affects the human body.

   .... [2]

   ii. Explain why AIDS and gonorrhoea cannot be treated by the same drugs.

   .... [2]

1. Tongue rolling is an example of discontinuous variation. It is partly controlled by a dominant allele, R, of a single gene.

   a. i. Name one other example of discontinuous variation in humans.

   .... [1]

   ii. Define the term *allele*.

   .... [1]

   iii. Draw a simple labelled diagram to show how genes and chromosomes are related to one another.   [2]

   b. This diagram shows a family history (a pedigree) of tongue rolling over three generations.

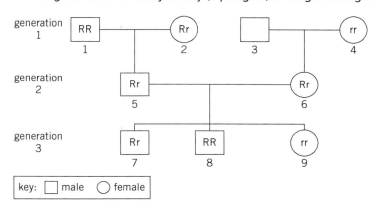

   i. State which individual in generation 3 is *not* a tongue roller. .... [1]

   ii. Suggest the possible genotypes of individual 3. .... [1]

   iii. Individual 7 marries a woman who is heterozygous for tongue rolling.

      State the probability (chance) that their second child will be a tongue roller.

   .... [1]

   c. Scientists often trace the inheritance of characteristics through mitochondrial DNA. Explain what is meant by mitochondrial DNA, and suggest why it provides evidence of inheritance through the maternal line only.

1. The diagram shows a short sequence of bases in a DNA molecule. The base sequence in DNA carries information in the form of a genetic code.

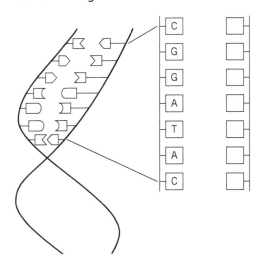

a. Write down the sequence of bases on the other strand of the DNA molecule. [2]

b. A modified copy of the DNA sequence is carried to the cytoplasm of the cell.

   i. State the name of this modified sequence. .... [1]

   ii. State the name of the structure in the cell where the code is 'read' by the cell. .... [1]

c. A sequence of three bases carries a code for another type of biological molecule.

   State the name of this type of molecule. .... [1]

d. The type of molecule named in your answer to part c. is built up into larger molecules, and these molecules determine the characteristics of organisms.

   i. State the general name given to these larger molecules. .... [1]

   ii. Complete this table to match the molecules to their functions (i.e. to the characteristics they give to an organism). [5]

Molecule	Characteristic
	Ability of red blood cells to transport oxygen
	Bind to and identify molecules on the surface of invading microbes
Receptor protein in synapse	
Lipase	
	Provides strength and structure to hair and nails

2. Look up what is meant by CrispR technology. Suggest how this technology might help in medicine.

1. The initials DNA stand for .... The structure of this

   molecule was discovered by two scientists, ... and .... in 1953. They were helped by

   the X-ray studies of ....

2. a. Here is a list of statements about DNA. State whether each of the statements is true or false.

statement	true	false
DNA carries coded instructions for the characteristics of an organism		
DNA is only found in the nucleus of cells of vertebrate animals		
DNA is a large molecule, but its code is carried in only four different subunits		
A DNA profile can be used to identify a criminal		
DNA can be extracted from dead dinosaurs		
Plant cells have different DNA to animal cells		
One difference between animals and bacteria is that bacteria do not have DNA		
The DNA profile is unique to each individual human		
50 human cheek cells fit into a 1 mm space, but each cheek cell contains 2 m of DNA		
Zoo scientists can copy the DNA found in an orang-utan, and check if it is related to an orang-utan at another zoo		

3. Genetic engineers can produce Golden Rice.

   State which **one** of the following is a benefit of this process   [1]

   A   the golden colour of the rice attracts pollinating insects

   B   the rice contains high levels of β-carotene, which can be converted to vitamin D

   C   the rice contains high levels of β-carotene, which can be converted to vitamin A

   D   the engineered rice is resistant to herbicide sprays

4. Here are three more statements about DNA. Working with two other people (so that there is an odd number in the group), discuss each of these statements. At the end of your discussion, take a vote to decide whether your group agrees or disagrees with the statement. Your teacher might ask you to explain your decision.

statement	agree	disagree
The police should be able to collect DNA from anyone in the country to use for checking crime scenes.		
A health insurance company has the right to check your DNA profile before giving you a life insurance policy.		
An adopted child should be able to use its DNA profile to track down its biological parents.		

Extension

1. Chromosomes contain DNA. Each individual, with very few exceptions, has different DNA. The DNA can be broken up, and the pieces used to produce a 'genetic fingerprint'. The diagram shows the genetic fingerprints of blood found at a murder scene and from blood samples provided by five suspect.

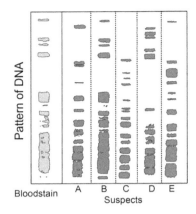

Fill in the missing words in the following sentences.

a. the chromosomes are found in the .... of the cell. [1]

b. genetic fingerprints must be made from the .... blood cells of the suspect [1]

c. the murderer was most likely to be suspect .... [1]

d. genetic fingerprints can only be identical if they come from .... [1]

e. Genetic fingerprinting can also be useful in other ways. Suggest how DNA fingerprinting could be valuable in

   i. prevention of dangerous inbreeding in rare animals kept in zoos.

   ....

   .... [2]

   ii. classification of living organisms collected from a new environment.

   ....

   .... [2]

f. DNA carries the code for protein synthesis.

   i. State which of the following is the correct sequence of events in this process.

      A mRNA→transcription→ translation→amino acid chain→DNA   B DNA→translation→mRNA→
      transcription→amino acid chain

      C DNA→transcription→mRNA→translation→amino acid chain   D amino acid chain→translation→
      mRNA→transcription→DNA

   ii. There are four different bases in DNA. A codon is made of three bases.

      State how many different codons can be produced..

1. Human body cells usually contain 23 pairs of chromosomes. The exceptions to this rule are the gametes and the mature red blood cells.

    a. Complete the table below.

Type of cell	Total number of chromosomes	Type of sex chromosomes present
Male nerve cell		
Female white blood cell		
Sperm cell		
Egg cell/ovum		
Red blood cell		

[5]

    b. Blood cells are produced in bone marrow. State the name of the type of cell division which produces them.

    .... [3]

2. When a baby is born it is possible to collect stem cells from the umbilical cord. The stem cells can be stored for many years at very low temperatures.

    a. i. Choose the **best** definition of stem cells.

        A Stem cells are specialised cells and join together to make unspecialised tissues.

        B Stem cells are unspecialised cells and divide to make specialised tissues.

        C Stem cells are unspecialised cells and join together to make specialised tissues.

        D Stem cells are specialised cells that divide and develop into unspecialised tissues.   [1]

       ii. Doctors believe that they can use the stored stem cells to treat diseases the baby might develop in the future.

        Choose the most likely way doctors might use the stem cells to treat heart disease.

        A They will produce a medicine for heart disease from the stem cells.

        B They will inject stem cells into the patient's bloodstream.

        C They will make a heart disease vaccine from the stem cells.

        D They will grow heart muscle cells from the stem cells.   [1]

    b. Umbilical cord blood provides **one** source of stem cells. Name one other source of stem cells.

    .... [1]

Extension

3. Methotrexate is a drug used to slow down the division of some human cells, for example in the treatment of some cancers. Suggest why doctors insist on regular blood tests for people being treated with this drug.

1. The photomicrograph shows a set of chromosomes during meiosis.

a. Complete the diagram below by drawing in the chromosomes of the four cells produced when the original cell divides by meiosis.

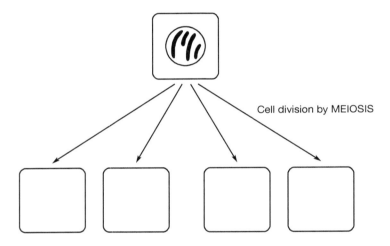

Cell division by MEIOSIS

[4]

b. State the site of meiosis in:

i. a mammal .... [1]

ii. a flowering plant. .... [1]

c. Explain why it is necessary for gametes to be produced by meiosis.

....

....

.... [2]

Extension

2. Meiosis takes place in a series of stages. Try to find images showing the behaviour of the chromosomes during meiosis. Explain how this process makes it very unlikely that there is any person (other than an identical twin) who has the same genotype as you.

1. This paragraph describes some features of inheritance.

    Use words from this list to complete each of the spaces in the paragraph. Each word may be used once, or not at all.

    allele   diploid   discontinuous   dominant   fertilisation   gene   haploid heterozygous   homozygous   meiosis   mitosis   recessive   redundant

    In humans, eye colour may be brown or blue. This is controlled by a single .... which has two forms.

    Gametes are formed by the type of cell division called .... : the gametes are

    .... and fuse at .... to form a

    .... zygote.

    Two humans both have brown eyes, but one of their three children has blue eyes. This means that blue eye colour is

    controlled by a .... allele and that both of the parents are .... [7]

2. Study the two lists below. One is a list of genetic terms and the other is a list of definitions of these terms.

    Draw guidelines to link each term with its correct definition.

Genetic term		Definition
Genotype		The observable features of an organism
Homozygous		An allele that is always expressed if it is present
Dominant		Having two alternative alleles of a gene
Heterozygous		One alternative form of a gene
Recessive		The set of alleles present in an organism
Chromosome		Having two identical alleles
Allele		A thread-like structure of DNA, carrying genetic information in the form of genes
Phenotype		Two identical alleles of a particular gene

[8]

3. Some closely related mammals, such as a horse and a donkey, can produce offspring. Suggest why these offspring are very rarely fertile.

1. A set of triplets was born, but their mother died during the birth. The babies were separated from one another, and brought up by different families. When they were 18 they met up with one another for the first time since their separation. Various measurements were made on them, and some of the information obtained is recorded in this table.

	Andrew	John	David
Mass / kg	81	92	86
Height / cm	179	180	179
Blood group	O	O	AB
Intelligence quotient (IQ)	128	138	140

a. i. State which two of the boys might be identical twins from this evidence.

.... and .... [1]

ii. Explain which piece of evidence is most important in helping you to reach this conclusion.

....

.... [1]

iii. Suggest a reason why Andrew and David have such different body mass measurements although they are of the same height.

.... [1]

b. The ABO blood group is determined by three alleles, although only two are present in any one cell. The three alleles are given the symbols I^A, I^B, and I^O.

The relationship between genotype and phenotype for these blood groups is shown in the table below.

Genotype	$I^A I^A$	$I^A I^O$	$I^B I^B$	$I^B I^O$	$I^A I^B$	$I^O I^O$
Phenotype	A	A	B	B	AB	O

State the name of this type of genetic relationship, in which a particular combination of alleles (in this case $I^A I^B$) results in a new phenotype.

.... [1]

2. Draw a Punnett square to suggest how two pink-flowered plants can produce red, pink, and white flowers among their offspring.

Extension

1. Cystic fibrosis is an inherited disorder that affects the production of mucus and sweat. The mucus is not liquid enough, so is very sticky. It can block air passages in the lungs, and also the ducts from the pancreas and, in males, the testes.

   The condition is caused by a recessive allele.

   The diagram shows a family tree.

   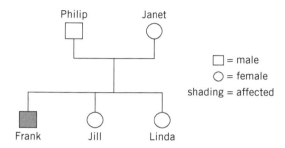

   = male
   = female
   shading = affected

   a. Suggest appropriate symbols for the dominant allele and for the recessive allele.

      Dominant .... Recessive .... [1]

   b. Use these symbols to give the genotype of the two parents.

      Philip .... Janet .... [2]

   c. State the possible genotypes of **i.** Frank .... and

                                        ii. Linda .... [2]

   d. If Philip and Janet decide to have another child, what is the probability that it will be affected by cystic fibrosis?

      .... [1]

   e. The pancreas releases a lipase and several proteases.

      Explain why a child with cystic fibrosis often grows and develops more slowly than a child without the condition.

      ....

      ....

      .... [3]

Extension

2. Find out about the patterns of inheritance for **Tay-Sachs disease** and for **achondroplasia**.

1. Haemophilia is a sex-linked inherited disease. It is controlled by alleles carried on the X chromosome (**H** for normal clotting, **h** for haemophilia).

The table below gives some information about possible combinations of phenotype and genotype.

Complete the table by:

a. drawing the correct chromosomes in boxes 2, 3, and 5

b. adding the symbols for the alleles to the correct positions on the chromosomes

c. writing into the final row the sex of each individual.

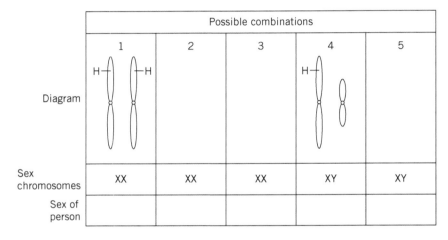

Possible combinations				
1	2	3	4	5
Diagram				
XX	XX	XX	XY	XY

Sex chromosomes / Sex of person   [5]

d. The genotype of individuals showing the normal clotting condition can be represented as:

Normal male $X^H Y$ Normal female $X^H X^H$

i. State the genotype of a carrier female ....   [1]

ii. Complete the Punnett Square below to show the results of a cross between a carrier female and a normal male

Gametes Female Male		

[4]

iii. What is the probability that a child from such a cross would be a male haemophiliac?

.... [1]

2. Very rarely the separation of X and Y chromosomes at meiosis does not take place properly, and a gamete may receive an unusual number of sex chromosomes. Suggest the likely characteristics of an individual with an XYY genotype. Suggest why lawyers may use an XYY genotype as a reason for some criminal behaviour.

1. Study the two lists below. One is a list of terms relating to variation and the other is a list of definitions of these terms.

   Draw guidelines to link each term with its correct definition.

Genetic term
Continuous variation
Gene
Discontinuous variation
Phenotype
Height in humans
Environment
Nutrients
Blood group

Definition
The observable features of an organism
A form of variation with many intermediate forms between the extremes
One possible form of environmental influence on variation
One example of discontinuous variation
This factor, in addition to genotype, can affect phenotype
A section of DNA responsible for an inherited characteristic
One example of continuous variation
A form of variation with clear-cut differences between groups

[8]

2. Charles Darwin believed that new **species** can arise by natural selection of variations within a population. Since Darwin's time, scientists have suggested that variation may arise by **mutation**, as well as by the formation of new combinations of **genes** at fertilisation during sexual reproduction.

   a. State the meanings of the terms:

   i. species .... [1]

   ii. mutation .... [1]

   iii. gene .... [1]

   b. Suggest **two** factors that may increase the rate of mutation in a population.

   1. ....

   2. .... [2]

3. Actors sometimes need to change their appearance in order to play a part in a film production. Both hair and eye colour are frequently altered to fit into a specific role. Use the terms phenotype and genotype to explain how they might make these changes.

Extension

1. a. The table below shows some examples of selection.

Example	Type of selection: natural or artificial
Cattle being bred that are able to withstand cold winters	
The development of a strain of rice that is more resistant to disease	
The resistance of a strain of bacteria to a particular antibiotic	
The ability of a species of shrub to grow on soil containing high amounts of copper	
The similarity between a moth's wing pattern and its habitat, making it less conspicuous to predatory birds	

Complete the table to show which type of selection, natural or artificial, is involved.   [5]

b. The bar graph shows the average milk yield for a herd of Friesian cows between 1976 and 2004.

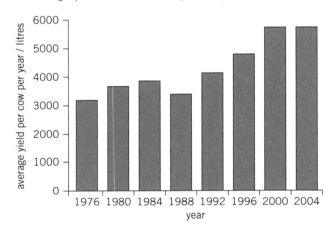

i. Explain how animal breeders might have caused the trend between 1976 and 2004 to occur.

....

....

.... [4]

ii. Apart from the yield of food (milk or meat), suggest another characteristic that farmers might improve in animals to make a farm more economically successful.

.... [1]

Extension

2. One animal studied by Charles Darwin was the great spotted woodpecker (*Dendrocopos major*). Make a drawing to show the adaptations of this bird to its way of life.

1. The Everglades is an enormous flooded area in southern Florida, USA.

   There are many different species of animals and plants there, and they are well adapted to their environment.

   a. The animals and plants have become well adapted by the process of natural selection.

      The following are stages in the evolution of species by means of natural selection.

      A survival of the best adapted

      B over-production of offspring

      C competition causes a struggle for existence

      D advantageous characteristics are passed on to offspring

      E variation occurs between members of the same population

      Use the letters **A–E** to rearrange these stages into the correct sequence.

      …..   …..   …..   …..   …..   [5]

   b. Some of the early European explorers in Florida noticed that there were many species of bird.

      The heads and beaks of birds are often well adapted to their diet. The diagrams in this table show the heads of some species of birds.

      Draw guidelines to match up the heads with the likely diet of the birds.

    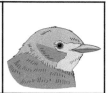

Feeds on nuts and other hard fruits	Filters algae and other small organisms from the water	Feeds by spearing fish and frogs	Captures Florida rabbits and other mammals	Feeds by catching small insects

[5]

2. Find out who Trofim Lysenko was. How did his ideas on evolution differ from those of Charles Darwin?

117

1. The diagrams below show the effect of selective breeding on wild cabbage (*Brassica oleracea*).

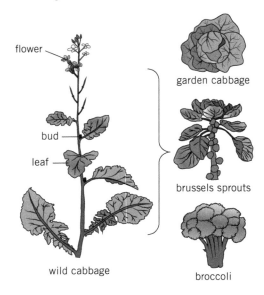

flower

bud

leaf

wild cabbage

garden cabbage

brussels sprouts

broccoli

a. State which part of the wild cabbage has been selected for when breeding the:

brussels sprouts ....

broccoli .... [2]

b. Once a plant has been selected as a new variety of broccoli, the grower then produces many more identical plants by taking cuttings.

i. Explain why the cuttings grow to be identical to the parent plant.

....

....

.... [2]

ii. The cuttings are usually planted into a type of compost containing plant hormones (to encourage rooting) and additional nitrate. The cuttings are kept in a closed transparent enclosure.

Explain the importance of:

nitrate in the growth compost ....

.... [1]

keeping the plants in a closed environment. ....

.... [1]

2. Make an internet search to find an image (or group of images) that could be used to illustrate how artificial selection could produce a springer spaniel from an ancestral wolf.

1. David and Salim were working together on a mathematical investigation. They decided to measure the body masses of each of the other students in their class.

The results are shown in this table.

Mass category / kg	Tally of number in group	Number in group
35–38	I	
39–42	II	
43–46	IIII	
47–50	IIII I	
51–54	IIII IIII	
55–58	IIII	
59–62	III	
63–66	II	
67–70	I	

a. Complete the third column of the table by adding up the tally numbers. [2]

b. Plot these results in a suitable form on the grid below.

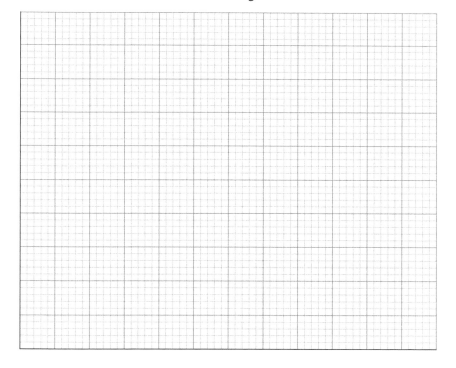

[5]

c. State which form of variation this graph illustrates. .... [1]

d. Explain how this form of variation comes about. ....

.... [2]

1. A student used a 50 cm quadrat to investigate the distribution of small arthropods called springtails in the leaf litter of a woodland. The number of springtails in each quadrat is shown in the diagram.

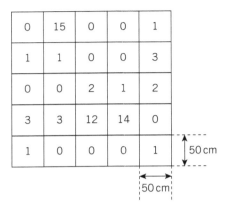

0	15	0	0	1
1	1	0	0	3
0	0	2	1	2
3	3	12	14	0
1	0	0	0	1

50 cm

50 cm

a. Calculate the area of each quadrat.

.... m² [1]

b. Calculate the mean number of springtails per square metre in the area studied by this student. Show your working.

Mean number of springtails per square metre = ... [2]

c. The springtails were not evenly distributed in the woodland. They were found mainly under pieces of dead wood.

Suggest **two** advantages to springtails of living underneath the pieces of dead wood.

1. ....

2. .... [2]

Extension

2. Zookeepers try to copy an animal's environment as closely as possible when they design a modern zoo enclosure. Suggest what should be included in their design if they are to try to breed animals for release into the wild.

1. Use guide lines to match the terms with their definitions.

Term/process		Definition
Food chain		An organism that gets its energy from dead or waste organic material
Food web		An organism that gets its energy by feeding on other organisms
Producer		An animal that gets its energy by eating other animals
Consumer		A network of interconnected food chains
Herbivore		The transfer of energy from one organism to the next, beginning with a producer
Carnivore		An organism that makes its own organic nutrients, usually through photosynthesis
Decomposer		An animal that gets its energy from eating plants

2. A group of students studied a food web for an English lake.

Algae are small microscopic plants. Water fleas are small crustaceans about 2 mm in length. Smelt are fish – they are adult at about 4 cm in length. The kingfisher is a bird, about 22 cm long.

Draw and label a likely pyramid of numbers for the food chain linking:

algae ⟶ water fleas ⟶ smelt ⟶ kingfisher

[2]

Extension

3. An efficient plant can convert about 10% of the light energy that falls on it into chemical energy. Find out the efficiency of a solar panel in the conversion of light to electrical energy.

121

1. The diagram shows a food web for an English lake.

   a. Write out a food chain involving five organisms from the lake.

[2]

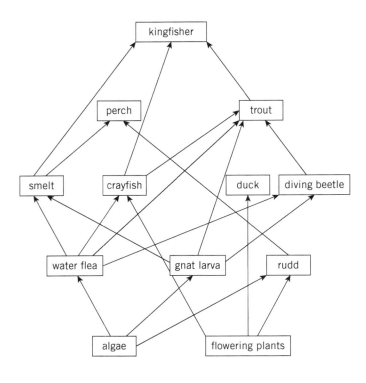

   b. Name **two** predators of gnat larvae

      1. ....

      2. .... [2]

   c. Algae are small microscopic plants. Water fleas are small crustaceans about 2mm in length. Smelt are fish – they are adult at about 4 cm in length. The kingfisher is a bird, about 22 cm long.

      Draw and label a likely pyramid of numbers for the food chain linking

[2]

   d. Suggest the changes that might occur if the gnat larvae were killed (by pesticide, for example).

1. a. This diagram represents the energy flow through a food chain.

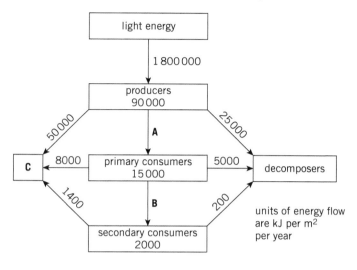

i. Name the source of light energy. .... [1]

ii. State the process occurring at **A** and **B**. .... [1]

iii. Explain why not all of the light energy available is absorbed by the producers.

....

.... [2]

iv. State the name of the process shown at **C**, and the form in which the energy is lost.

Process .... [1]

Form of energy lost .... [1]

b. i. Calculate the percentage of energy transferred at stages **A** and **B**.

Show your working.

A .... **B** .... [2]

ii. Suggest how evidence in the diagram supports the idea that humans should eat more vegetable matter and less meat.

....

....

....

.... [3]

2. What is a **pyramid of biomass**? Suggest why an ecologist would be more interested in a pyramid of biomass than in a pyramid of numbers.

1. A group of students decided to investigate the decay of leaves.

   Four samples of equal masses of leaves were placed in bags made of plastic mesh.

   The mesh size in bags **A**, **B**, and **C** was the same, but the mesh size in bag **D** was much smaller.

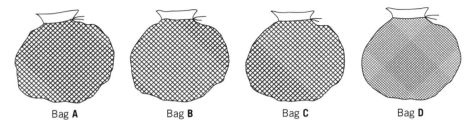

   Bag **A**   Bag **B**   Bag **C**   Bag **D**

   - The bags of leaves were weighed.
   - The bags were buried at the same depth in different soils.
   - The bags were kept at the same temperature.
   - After 100 days the bags were dug up and reweighed.

   The results of the investigation are shown in this table.

Bag	Location	Type of soil	Mass at start / g	Mass after 100 days / g	Loss of mass / g
A	Garden	Wet clay	60	58	2
B	Woodland	Dry, sandy	60	51	9
C	Woodland	Moist	60	32	
D	Woodland	Moist	60	43	

   a. i. Complete the table to show the loss in mass in bags **C** and **D**. [1]

      ii. Explain how the results suggest that decay requires water and air (oxygen) to take place.

      ....

      .... [2]

      iii. Explain the difference between the results for bags **C** and **D**.

      .... [1]

      iv. Explain why it was important that the bags were made of plastic.

      .... [1]

   b. State the names of **two** types of organism responsible for decay.

      .... [2]

2. Wood is a natural product, and has been used for more than a hundred years in the manufacture of railway sleepers and telegraph poles. Railway builders in East Africa found that wooden products were quickly destroyed by both termites and decomposing microbes. Suggest how humans can protect wood against decomposers.

1. The first part of this question asks you to use a list of words to fill in a set of boxes. This is quite a common way to test your knowledge and understanding of a biological process. The diagram below represents the carbon cycle.

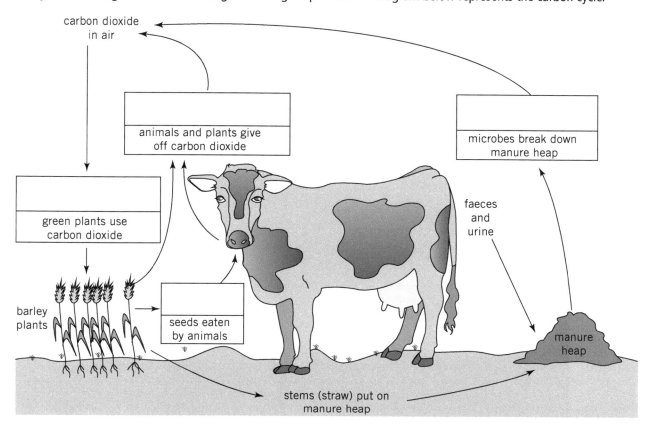

a. Use words from this list to complete the boxes in the diagram.

combustion   decay   excretion   feeding   photosynthesis   respiration   [4]

b. In some countries the manure heap is collected, dried, and then burned as a fuel.

State the effect that this would have on the carbon dioxide concentration in the air.

.... [1]

Extension

2. Commercial businesses now often advertise that they plant trees to reduce their carbon footprint. Explain what is meant by a carbon footprint. Calculate the carbon footprint of your family's transport requirements (cars and aeroplanes) over the past year.

1. a. The diagram shows the nitrogen cycle.

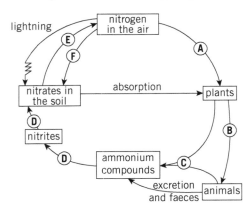

i. Name the processes **B** and **E**.

B ....

E .... [2]

ii. Name the process and the organisms involved in **C**.

Process ....

Organisms .... [2]

b. A heap of dead leaves had been left to decompose. Part of the decomposition sequence is shown below.

| dead leaves | decomposers → | ammonium | *Nitrosomonas* bacteria → | nitrite | *Nitrobacter* bacteria → | nitrate |

Use this sequence and your own knowledge to answer the following questions.

i. Suggest **three** effects on the sequence if the *Nitrosomonas* bacteria died out.

1. ....

2. ....

3. .... [3]

ii. Tick **two** boxes in this table to show factors which would speed up the decomposition process.

Factor	Box
Maintaining an acid pH	
A plastic cover to exclude air	
Few scavenging insects	
Many scavenging insects	
Regular turning of the heap to add air	

[2]

Extension

2. Explain how root nodules illustrate the principle of symbiosis.

1. This diagram shows a number of factors that can affect the size of a population.

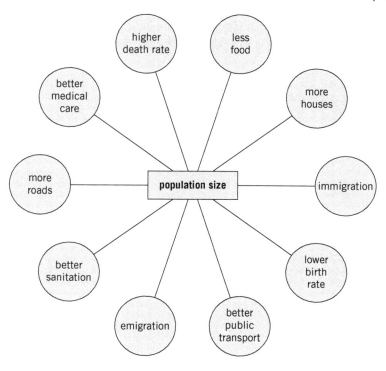

a. State **four** factors, shown in the diagram, that reduce the size of a population.

....

....

....

.... [4]

b. Suggest **two** ways in which better medical care can lead to an increase in the size of a population.

....

.... [2]

c. State **two** ways in which humans control bacterial populations.   [1]

....

.... [2]

2. The rose-ringed parakeet (*Psittacula krameri*) is an 'alien' to Britain. The population in the wild was probably no more than 30–50 in the 1980s. What is its population now? Explain why its population has increased so rapidly.

1. An experiment was carried out to follow the population growth of the bacterium *Escherichia coli*.

Cells of the bacterium were placed in a flask containing sterile nutrient broth and then incubated at 30 °C. Every five hours a sample was removed from the flask, and the number of bacteria present was calculated.

The results are shown in this table.

Time from start / h	5	10	15	20	25	30	35	40	45	50
Number of bacteria / millions per cm³	20	50	430	450	460	420	220	55	20	0

a. Draw a graph of these results on the grid below.

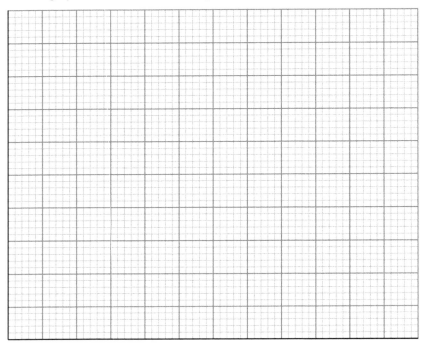

b. Suggest why the nutrient broth:

contains sugar .... [1]

contains amino acids .... [1]

must be sterile. ....

.... [2]

c. Mark with a letter **R** on the graph the period during the experiment when the rate of reproduction was at its greatest. [1]

d. Suggest **two** possible reasons why the population declined between 25 and 50 hours. [1]

....

.... [2]

1. a. The following table gives a list of some terms associated with genetic engineering, and some definitions for these terms.

   Match the terms in column 1 with the correct definition from column 2.

Term		Definition
Gene		A small circle of DNA in a bacterial cell
Plasmid		An enzyme that can splice one gene into another section of DNA
Vector		An enzyme that can cut out a specific gene from a chromosome
Ligase		Pieces of single-stranded DNA left exposed after a gene is removed from a chromosome
Restriction		A section of DNA coding for a protein
Sticky ends		A vessel in which engineered bacteria can produce a valuable product under optimum conditions
Fermenter		A structure which can carry a gene into another cell

   [6]

   b. Genetic engineering can be used to produce protein products that are useful to humans.

   State **one** reason why each of the following proteins is useful to humans.

   1. Insulin ....

   ....

   2. Factor 8 ....

   ....

   3. Pectinase ....

   ....

   4. Human growth hormone ....

   .... [4]

   c. Before the development of genetic engineering, vaccines were made by heating or chemically treating whole viruses. The vaccine therefore contained whole virus particles.

   Explain why it is safer to use a genetically engineered vaccine rather than one made directly from the hepatitis B virus.

   ....

   ....

   .... [2]

Extension

2. Explain how gene therapy may provide a treatment for retinal macular degeneration.

1. The table below shows the energy content and the concentration of insecticide in a group of organisms in a food chain.

Organism in food chain	Energy content / percentage of original energy	Concentration of insecticide in body / mg per kg
Human	1	1.5
Food fish	3	0.1
Small fish	9	0.03
Microscopic animals	20	0.01
Algae (microscopic plants)	100	0.001

a. Calculate the percentage of energy loss between the microscopic plants and the food fish.

.... % [1]

b. Using information from the table, explain why food chains involving humans should be kept as short as possible.

....

.... [2]

c. Describe **one** way in which insecticides have been harmful to organisms other than the target insects.

....

.... [2]

d. Genetic engineers can produce crop plants which are resistant to pesticides. It means that they can spray pesticides without risking damage to their crops.

Outline the steps needed to produce a pesticide-tolerant plant.

....

....

....

.... [4]

2. What is a molluscicide? Explain how the spread of one disease-causing organism can be controlled by the use of a molluscicide.

1. More food and raw materials are required to meet the demands of an increasing world population.

   Describe and explain the possible harmful effects on organisms and the environment of burning large areas of Indonesian rainforest, so that the land can be used to grow palm oil trees.

   ....

   ....

   ....

   .... [4]

2. These diagrams show changes to a farm between 1953 and 2003.

   The fields on the farm are separated by hedges.

   a. i. State **two** major changes which were made to the land between 1953 and 2003.

      1. ....

      2. .... [2]

      ii. Suggest and explain **two** ways in which these changes would affect wildlife on the farm.

      1. ....

      ....

      2. ....

      .... [4]

   b. Farmers often remove areas of woodland to provide more space for growing crops.

      Suggest **three** disadvantages of this deforestation.

      1. ....

      2. ....

      3. .... [3]

3. A recent survey of the grey partridge (*Perdix perdix*) in Britain found that its population was declining rapidly. Ecologists suggested that this was due to agricultural practices used in the UK. Explain how modern agriculture might have caused this population decline. Suggest how it could be reversed.

Extension

1. a. This set of pie charts shows the food groups present in eggs, milk, rice, and beans.

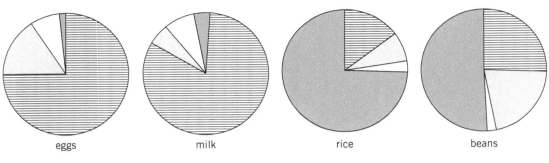

eggs   milk   rice   beans

key to food groups
▤ water   ☐ proteins   ☐ fats and oils   ▦ carbohydrates

A malnourished person may have an unbalanced diet that may be missing some essential nutrients.

i. State which food has the highest concentration of protein. .... [1]

ii. State which food has the most carbohydrate. .... [1]

iii. Name **two** other food groups not shown in the pie charts.

....

.... [2]

b. An extreme and continued shortage of food can result in a famine.

State **three** factors which may cause this shortage of food.

1. ....

2. ....

3. .... [3]

2. Some people suggest that wealthy countries should not provide food for people living in desert areas, as these areas can never supply enough food to support a large human population. These people say that this food support will have to go on indefinitely, and that the population should be allowed to 'balance' to what the environment can provide. What do you think?

1. The table below provides some data about a number of atmospheric gases.

Name of gas	Source(s) of gas	Percentage influence on greenhouse effect
CFCs	Air conditioning systems; aerosol propellant; refrigerators	13
Carbon dioxide	Burning forest trees; burning fossil fuels; production of cement	56
Nitrous oxide	Breakdown of fertilisers	6
Methane	Waste gases from animals such as sheep, cattle, and termites; rotting vegetation	25

a. Explain why these gases are called 'greenhouse' gases.

....

....

.... [2]

b. From this data suggest why the following practices should be encouraged:

   i. Development of renewable energy resources such as wind turbines.

   .... [1]

   ii. Improved insulation of walls and roofs in houses.

   .... [1]

   iii. Reforestation.

   .... [1]

2. There are large copper mines in Tanzania. One of these mines is so far from railway links that all supplies must be brought in, and all products and waste materials removed, by trucks. These trucks run throughout the day and night.

   Describe and explain the possible harmful effects on organisms and the environment.

   ....

   ....

   .... [3]

3. Recent research has shown that some car manufacturers have been providing false information about the emission of PM. Explain what PM is, and why it is dangerous to health.

1. Organisms in a lake or river can be affected by pollution. The statements below describe some of the effects on organisms of sewage being allowed to run into the water.

   The statements are in the wrong order.

Statement	Letter
Plants on the bottom of the lake die	A
Algae near the surface of the lake absorb nitrates and grow in large numbers	B
Sewage flows into the lake from a nearby farm	C
Increased algae prevent light from reaching plants rooted at the bottom of the lake	D
Bacteria break down the sewage into nitrates	E

   a. Rearrange the letters to show the correct sequence of events. The first one has been done for you.

Sequence of events	First step	Second step	Third step	Fourth step	Fifth step
Letter	C				

   [4]

   b. Suggest one other source of nitrates which may enter the lake.

   .... [1]

   c. The sequence that you have described in your answer to part **a.** is not the end of the harmful events that may take place.

   Describe **three** further steps to show how aerobic bacteria may cause the death of fish and larger invertebrates in the lake.

   1. ....

   2. ....

   3. .... [3]

2. One of the effects of eutrophication is that polluted water can be harmful to human babies. Suggest why this could happen.

1. Define the term *conservation*. ....

   .... [2]

2. a. The giant panda (*Ailuropoda melanoleuca*) is an endangered species.

   i. Suggest and explain **two** reasons why the panda is endangered. One reason should relate to the environment, and one reason should relate to the biology of the panda itself.

      Environmental factor .... Explanation of effect ....

      .... [2]

      Biological factor .... Explanation of effect ....

      .... [2]

   ii. The giant panda is sometimes called a **flagship species**. Explain what is meant by a flagship species.

       ....

       .... [2]

   b. A conservation management plan involves several steps. The first step is to sample the population of the endangered species.

   i. Explain why sampling is necessary. ....

      .... [2]

   ii. For any named species, suggest a suitable method of sampling.

       Name of species ....

       Method of sampling ....

       .... [2]

   c. Recent population surveys suggest that the hedgehog (*Erinaceus europaeus*) is very quickly declining in numbers. Some conservationists suggest that the badger (*Meles meles*) is to blame. Suggest what can be done to reverse this fall in hedgehog populations.

1. Modern fishing boats use ultrasound equipment to locate shoals of fish, and giant nets with very small mesh to capture their prey.

   Describe and explain the possible harmful effects on organisms and the environment.

   ....

   ....

   ....

   ....

   ....

   .... [3]

2. Until recent times, fishing to the north-east of the UK was largely unrestricted.

   Suggest **three** measures that could be taken to help to conserve the cod population in this area.

   1. ....

   ....

   ....

   2. ....

   ....

   ....

   3. ....

   ....

   .... [3]

Extension

3. The Chinese government is building artificial islands on coral atolls in the South China Sea. Conservationists are anxious that this work will affect fish populations in that part of the world. Explain how this could happen.

1. A farmer believes in **sustainable** farming.

   a. What is meant by the term **sustainable**? ....

   .... [1]

   The farmer plants a forest of young fir trees. Ten years later the forest is thinned by removing some of the trees. A small part of the forest is harvested in each of the following years.

   b. Suggest **two** advantages of thinning the forest.

   ....

   .... [2]

   c. Suggest **two** disadvantages of growing trees as a monoculture.

   ....

   .... [2]

   d. This list contains some properties of trees. A farmer buying young trees would consider these properties when making his purchase.

   fast growth   **good growth on poor soil**   **high quality wood for pulp**

   low cost   **resistance to disease**

   Choose any **three** of these properties and suggest a reason why each property would be useful to the farmer.

Property	Reason for choice

Extension

2. Explain why some users of oriental medicine believe that it is acceptable to **a**. kill rhinoceros and **b**. keep bears in small cages.

1. Biotechnology has made it possible to use algae as a source of fuel.

   The algae are grown in a vessel called a biocoil, then dried and ground up to form a powder, which can be used as fuel.

   The biocoil is a transparent tube about 5 m high, and the algae constantly circulate through it in a nutrient solution. The algae grow and multiply at a very fast rate.

   The diagram shows the main stages in this process.

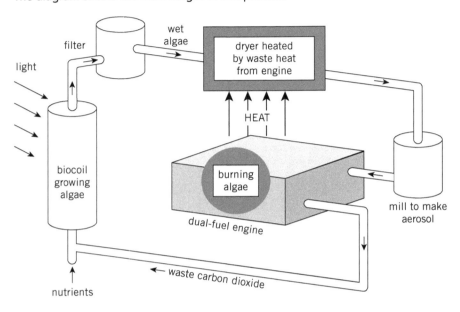

   a. Write out an equation to summarise how energy is trapped by the algae. [2]

   b. Explain why it is essential that the biocoil is transparent.

   ....

   ....

   .... [2]

   c. Explain why it is essential to use an organism with a high rate of reproduction in this process.

   ....

   ....

   .... [2]

2. Explain what is meant by 'fracking'.

   Suggest **two** possible benefits of this process, and **two** reasons why we might be anxious about the development of this industry.

1. a. The diagram shows some of the stages in paper manufacture and recycling.

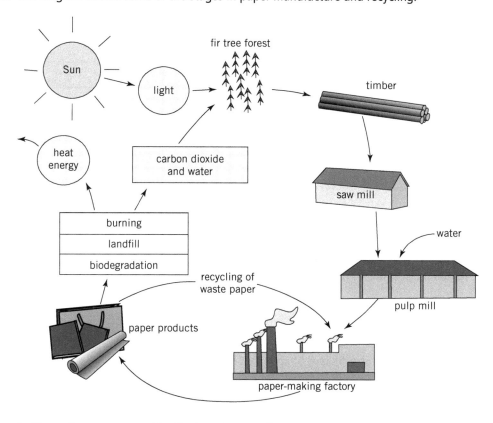

   i. Name the process used by the trees to manufacture sugars.

   .... [1]

   ii. Name the process by which carbon dioxide leaves the trees.

   .... [1]

   iii. In the mill the wood pulp is treated with sodium hydroxide to break down the fibres in the wood.

   State the effect on the pH of the pulp. .... [1]

   b. i. One of the paper products manufactured in the paper-making factory is paper bags. Give **two** reasons why paper bags are more environmentally friendly than plastic bags.

   ....

   .... [2]

   ii. Suggest **two** other uses of recycled waste paper.

   ....

   .... [2]

Extension

2. Assume that a soft drink can is composed of 100% aluminium, and that the mass of an Airbus-380 is 50% aluminium. Calculate how many soft drink cans would be needed to produce one Airbus-380. Consider where the aluminium would come from if it wasn't recycled.

1. a. For each of the following statements, mark as True (T) or False (F).

	Statement	True or False
1	A typical bacterium is about one thousandth of a metre wide	
2	Bacteria are smaller than viruses	
3	Gonorrhoea is caused by a bacterium	
4	Bacteria may contain plasmids	
5	All bacteria are harmful	
6	Bacteria multiply by binary fission	
7	A bacterium called *Vibrio* causes cholera	
8	Bacteria can produce the enzyme protease	
9	Bacteria can be genetically modified to produce human insulin	
10	Some bacteria can produce their own organic chemicals using energy from the Sun	
11	Bacteria in the human intestine produce some of the vitamins required for human health	
12	Bacteria have a nucleus, but it is smaller than a human nucleus	

[12]

b. For any three of the statements which you have labelled as False, explain why you have made that choice. [1]

1. Statement ....

Explanation ....

.... [2]

2. Statement ....

Explanation ....

.... [2]

3. Statement ....

Explanation ....

.... [2]

Extension

2. It is theoretically possible that a single bacterium in the human gut could become 2^{72} cells in a 24-hour period. Suggest why this doesn't happen.

1. The diagram shows a bioreactor used for the production of penicillin.

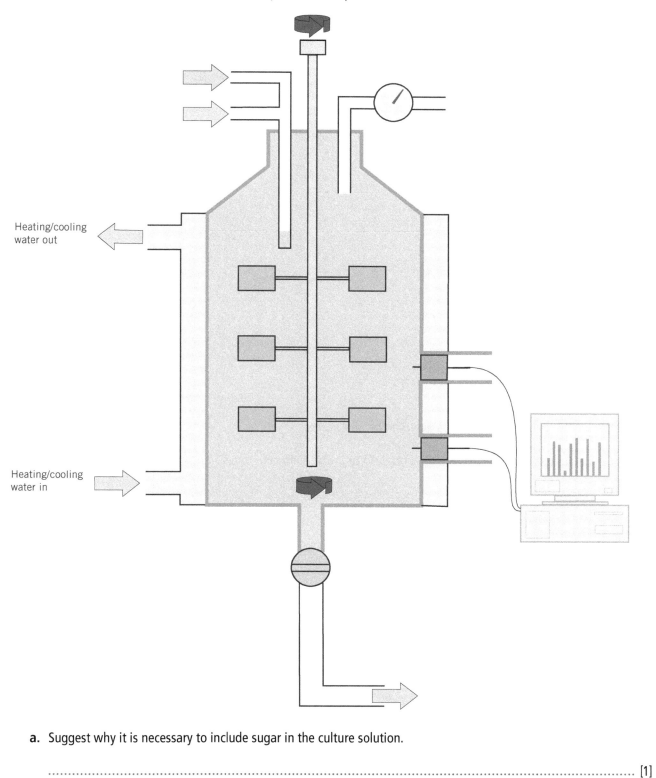

Heating/cooling water out

Heating/cooling water in

a. Suggest why it is necessary to include sugar in the culture solution.

.... [1]

b. It is necessary to maintain a constant temperature inside the bioreactor. Explain **why** this is necessary.

....

.... [2]

141

c. This graph shows the amounts of *Penicillium* fungus and penicillin in the bioreactor over a period of nine days.

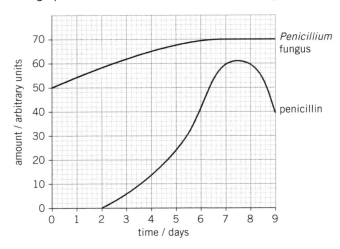

Suggest the best time to collect the penicillin.

....

Explain your answer.

....

.... [2]

d. Doctors are reluctant to prescribe penicillin for all illnesses.

Explain how the overuse of antibiotics can lead to the development of resistant strains of bacteria.

....

....

....

....

.... [3]

e. Bioreactors may also be used in the production of enzymes.

Complete this table about commercially valuable enzymes. One section has been completed for you.

Name of enzyme	Commercial value
	Clearing fruit juices by digesting clumps of plant cells
Lipase from fungi	Improves chocolate flow when coating biscuits
	Part of biological washing powders – remove blood stains
Lactase	

f. What is MRSA? Explain why people are so concerned about MRSA. Suggest what people can do to limit the effects of MRSA.

1. Scientists in the brewing and baking industries are interested in the metabolism of yeast.

A group of scientists investigated the production of alcohol from four different sugars, **M, N, O,** and **P**. They set up apparatus as shown in diagram **A** for each of the different sugars. The length of the carbon dioxide bubble shown in diagram **B** was measured at five-minute intervals.

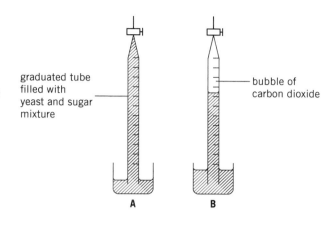

graduated tube filled with yeast and sugar mixture

bubble of carbon dioxide

A   B

- In each case the same concentration of sugar was used.

- The temperature was kept at 25°C throughout the experiments.

- This process is called alcoholic fermentation.

a. i. Explain the purpose of the yeast and sugar mixture. ....

.... [1]

ii. State the independent and dependent variables in this set of experiments.

independent ....

dependent .... [2]

iii. Explain why it is important that the tubes were **completely** filled with the mixture at the start of the experiments.

....

.... [1]

iv. Suggest why the rate of carbon dioxide production slowed down after about 25 minutes. ....

.... [2]

b. Write a word equation for the process of alcoholic fermentation.

[2]

c. Suggest **two** ways in which the rate of alcohol production could have been increased.

....

.... [2]

2. What are *Saccharomyces carlsbergensis* and *Candida utilis*? Explain why scientists would like to understand how to control the growth of these two organisms.

1. The diagram shows a piece of equipment used in one commercial use of enzymes.

Some enzymes are **immobilised** on a carrier of fibres. They can be re-used many times eg. lactase for lactose-free milk

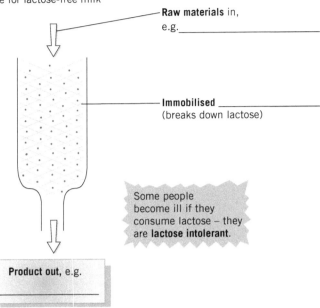

Raw materials in,
e.g._____

Immobilised _____
(breaks down lactose)

Some people become ill if they consume lactose – they are **lactose intolerant**.

Product out, e.g.
_____

a. Complete the diagram using words from this list.

amylase   lactase   milk containing lactose   lactose-free milk   starch

[3]

b. The enzyme is **immobilised** in this apparatus. Explain the meaning of the term immobilisation, and suggest why it is important in this process.

Meaning of term ....

Importance .... [2]

2. Research into the condition of **lactose intolerance**. What are the symptoms of this condition? How does lactose cause these problems?

Another condition associated with milk sugars is galactosaemia. Describe the symptoms of this condition

1. Pectinase and amylase are enzymes which break down different parts of plant cells.

   Two students carried out an investigation into the effect of these enzymes on fruit pulp made by crushing oranges in distilled water. The volumes and concentrations of the enzymes were constant. Tubes A, B and C were kept at room temperature (21°C), and tube D was kept at 30°C. The apparatus was left to stand for 24 hours.

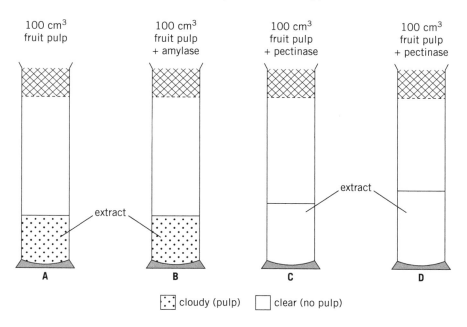

   The results are shown in the table below

	A	B	C	D
Volume of extract / cm³	22	23	40	55

   a. Calculate the volume of fruit pulp needed to produce 1000cm³ of clear extract if pectinase is used at room temperature. Show your working.

   [3]

   b. i. Explain the difference in appearance between tubes B and C.

      ....

      ....

      .... [2]

   ii. Explain the difference between the results for tubes C and D.

      ....

      ....

      .... [2]

Exam success: knowing what to do

Candidates taking an examination in IGCSE Biology are given instructions about what the examiner expects from them. These instructions are given in the introduction to each question, or to each part of a multi-part question. These instructions, which tell the candidate what to do, are given as **command words**.

For example, a candidate might be asked to **define** a biological term, to **describe** a biological process, or to **calculate** a numerical value. Define, describe, and calculate are command words. To be successful in an examination, a candidate must understand what each of the command words means.

Command words: what answer do you expect?

- Command words may require either concise answers or extended answers.

- Command words may require either recall or making logical connections between pieces of information.

- Some command words require only single word or single figure answers.

This list of the command words is taken from the IGCSE syllabus, published by CIE. The examination board stresses that these words are best understood when they are seen in an actual question, and they also point out that some other command words may be used. Even so, this list contains the most commonly used words and what they mean. In other words, these command words tell you what the examiner wants you to do when trying to answer a particular question.

Name: the answer is usually a technical term (diffusion, for example, or mitochondrion) consisting of no more than a few words. **State** is a very similar command word, although the answer may be longer, as a phrase or sentence. **Name** and **state** don't need anything added, i.e. *there is no need for an explanation*. Adding an explanation will take up time and probably won't gain any more marks!

---

a. State **three** normal functions of a root.

1. To anchor the plant in the soil ....

2. To absorb water from the soil ....

3. To absorb mineral ions from the soil ....

[3]

Define: the answer is a formal definition of a particular term. The answer is usually 'what is it' – for example, define the term active transport means 'what is active transport'.

Look carefully how many marks are offered. It is often a good idea to add an example to a definition – in this way the examiner can be sure that you know what you are trying to define.

What do you understand by or **what is meant by** are commands that also ask for a definition, but again the marks offered suggest that you should add some relevant comment on the importance of the terms concerned.

List: you need to write down a number of points, usually of only one word, with no need for explanation. For example, you might be asked to list four characteristics of living organisms.

Describe: your answer should simply say what is happening in a situation shown in the question, e.g. the number of germinating seeds increased to 55. There is no need for an explanation.

No call for explanation or comment ────

Make **three** points for the **three** marks on offer

c. (Describe) how water reaches a leaf and enters a palisade cell.

Evaporation/transpiration from leaf surface

water pulled up xylem to replace 'losses'

water moves by osmosis to palisade cell

water crosses palisade cell membrane by osmosis

[3]

d. (Describe) how sugar produced in a palisade cell reaches the roots.

Conversion to sucrose/transported in phloem/

unloaded in roots by diffusion or active transport

[2]

Explain: the answer will be in extended prose, i.e. in the form of complete sentences. You will need to use your knowledge and understanding of biological topics to write more about a statement that has been made in the question, or earlier in your answer.

The command word **explain** is often linked with **describe** or **state**, so that the examiner asks you to **describe and explain** or **state and explain**. This means that there are two parts to be answered – they can often be joined by the word 'because'. For example 'the number of germinating seeds increased to 55 (describe) because the temperature has increased and germination is controlled by enzymes which are sensitive to temperature (explain)'.

Many answers fail to gain full marks because they do not obey both commands – they often **describe** but do not **explain**, so only gain half of the available marks.

---

c. There is concern that pollution of the environment may change the breeding grounds of the Adelie penguin.

(State and explain) the effect this might have on the populations of the Leopard seal and the Ross seal.

two pieces of information needed – can you link them with the word 'because'?

Leopard seal Population could fall because there would

be less food for them (so they would breed

less successfully)

Ross seal Population could rise because there would

be fewer leopard seals to act as predators

[4]

Suggest: this command word has two possible meanings. In the first, you will need to use your biological knowledge and understanding to explain something that is new to you. You might use the principle of enzyme action (which you know about) to explain an industrial process (which might be new to you). Suggest also has a second meaning – it implies that that there may be more than one possible answer to a question. For example, there might be a number of different factors affecting the action of a digestive enzyme.

Questions which involve data response (like looking at a table of results, for example) and problem solving (like comparing three different environmental situations, for example) often begin with the command word **suggest**.

Calculate: a numerical answer is expected, usually obtained from data given in the question. Remember:

- Show your working (there may be marks given for the correct method even if you get the wrong answer).

- Give your answer to the correct number of significant figures, usually two or three.

- Give the correct units (if needed – sometimes these will already be given in the space left for your answer).

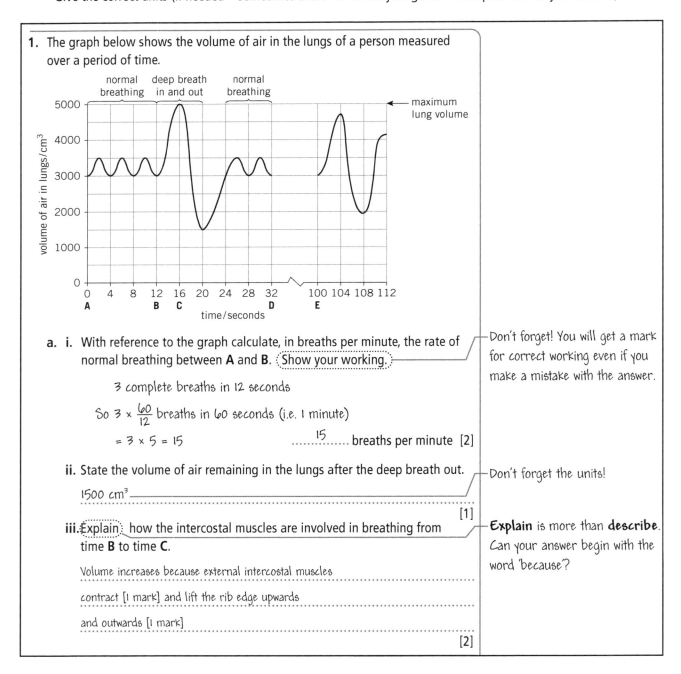

1. The graph below shows the volume of air in the lungs of a person measured over a period of time.

   a. i. With reference to the graph calculate, in breaths per minute, the rate of normal breathing between **A** and **B**. Show your working.

> *Don't forget! You will get a mark for correct working even if you make a mistake with the answer.*

       3 complete breaths in 12 seconds

       So $3 \times \frac{60}{12}$ breaths in 60 seconds (i.e. 1 minute)

       $= 3 \times 5 = 15$ ......15...... breaths per minute [2]

   ii. State the volume of air remaining in the lungs after the deep breath out.

> *Don't forget the units!*

       1500 cm³

       [1]

   iii. Explain how the intercostal muscles are involved in breathing from time **B** to time **C**.

> *Explain is more than describe. Can your answer begin with the word 'because'?*

       Volume increases because external intercostal muscles

       contract [1 mark] and lift the rib edge upwards

       and outwards [1 mark]

       [2]

Other terms which require numerical answers are **find**, **measure** and **determine**.

Find is a general term, and can mean calculate, measure or determine.

Measure implies that the answer can be obtained by a direct measurement, e.g. using a ruler to measure the length of a structure on a diagram.

Determine means that the quantity cannot be measured directly, but has to be obtained by calculation or from a graph. For example, the size of a cell from a scale included in the diagram of the cell.

The graph below shows the heart rate and the cardiac output. The cardiac output is the volume of blood pumped out of the heart each minute.

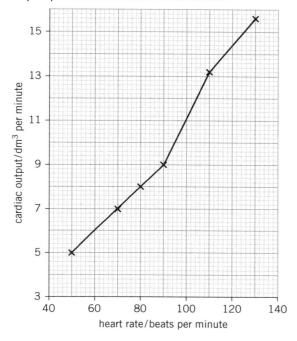

a. i. State the cardiac output at a heart rate of 100 beats per minute. ——————

     11 dm³ per minute ————————————————————————————

                                                                 [1]

   ii. Determine the increase in cardiac output when the heart rate increases from 70 to 90 beats per minute.

         7   9

     (9 − 7) = 2 .... dm³ per minute   [1]

  iii. Determine the increase in cardiac output when the heart rate increases from 100 to 120 beats per minute.

         11   14.4

     (14.4 − 11) = 3.4 .... dm³ per minute   [1]

read directly (and accurately!) from the graph

don't forget the units!

means the same as 'calculate' (or 'work out')

- Some questions cover complicated material but actually contain most of the information that you need to gain full marks!

7. **a.** Restriction endonucleases are enzymes used to cut DNA into fragments during genetic engineering. EcoR1 is a restriction enzyme produced by the bacterium *Escherichia coli*. It always cuts DNA at the same sequence of organic bases. The base sequence below shows some of the remaining organic bases after a cut.

> Write the missing bases in the correct position to show the DNA before the cut.

many candidates missed this instruction (and hence 1 mark)

[1]

*could be easily worked out as long as you noted the question 'gave' the pairing of G-C, the other base pair therefore **must** be A-T (or T-A)*

b. The diagram below represents a length of DNA after being treated with EcoR1 restriction endonucleases.

DNA fragments

Organic base pairs   21226   4878   5643   7421   5804   3530

i. State how many   C T T A A G   base sequences were on the original DNA molecule.

........5..

[1]

i.e. there were five points at which this enzyme could recognise and 'cut' the DNA

ii. Work out how many individual organic bases there are on the DNA shown.

........48502   ×   2 = 97 004..

[1]

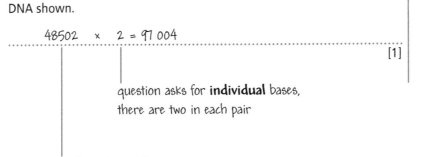

*question asks for **individual** bases, there are two in each pair*

*total number of **base** pairs*
(21226 + 4878 + 5643 + 7421 + 5804 + 3530)

c. The following table lists events from the identification of a human gene coding for a hormone "X" to the commercial production of hormone "X".

Genes can be transferred into plasmids, tiny circles of DNA which are found in bacteria.

Show the correct sequence of events 1 to 8 by writing the appropriate number in each box provided. The first (number 1) and last (number 8) have been completed for you.

follow very straightforwardly from number 1.

Event	Number
Cutting of a bacterial plasmid using restriction endonuclease	3
Cutting of human DNA with restriction endonuclease	2
Identification of the human DNA which codes for hormone "X"	1
Many identical plasmids, complete with human gene, are produced inside the bacterium	6
Mixing together human gene and "cut" plasmids to splice the human gene into the plasmid	4
Some of the cloned bacteria are put into an industrial fermenter where they breed and secrete the hormone	8
The bacterium is cloned	7
Using the plasmid as a vector, inserting it, complete with human gene, into a bacterium	5

clearly the step prior to number 8

Six marks gained by applying a logical and methodical approach to dealing with information supplied by the examiner.

[6]

Simple summary:

State, define, or **name**	What is it?
Describe	What is happening?
Explain	Why is it happening?
Calculate	How many or how big?

Check a copy of a recent IGCSE Biology Paper (0610 for example). Underline the command words. Which ones are used most often?

Exam-style questions

Multiple choice

Remember that there are two alternative multiple-choice papers. Paper 1 contains questions which only assess material from the **core** syllabus, paper 2 contains questions that could contain material from either the **core** or the **supplement**.

Sample 'core' questions

1. Root hair cells are found on plant roots.

   Which of the following features would be present in a root hair cell but not in a cell lining the small intestine?

   A cytoplasm   **B** chloroplasts

   C cell wall   **D** cell membrane

2. Which animal is a spider?

   1. has legs .... go to 2

        has no legs .... go to 3

   2. has six legs .... organism **A**

        has eight legs .... organism **B**

   3. has a shell .... organism **C**

        has no shell .... organism **D**

3. Dietary fibre passes through several structures after leaving the stomach.

   In which order does the dietary fibre pass through these structures?

   A ileum – duodenum – rectum – colon

   B duodenum – ileum – rectum – colon

   C ileum – duodenum – colon – rectum

   D duodenum – ileum – colon – rectum

4. Which chemical elements are found in carbohydrates, fats, and proteins?

	Carbohydrates	Fats	Proteins
A	Carbon, hydrogen, and oxygen	Carbon, hydrogen, and oxygen	Carbon, hydrogen, oxygen, and nitrogen
B	Carbon, hydrogen, and oxygen	Carbon, hydrogen, oxygen, and nitrogen	Carbon, hydrogen, and oxygen
C	Carbon, hydrogen, oxygen, and nitrogen	Carbon, hydrogen, and oxygen	Carbon, hydrogen, and oxygen
D	Carbon, hydrogen, oxygen, and nitrogen	Carbon, hydrogen, and oxygen	Carbon, hydrogen, oxygen, and nitrogen

5. Plant and animal cells have many common structures. State which of the following are present in plant cells but **not** in animal cells.

    A chloroplast and cell wall

    B cell membrane and chloroplast

    C cell membrane and nucleus

    D nucleus and cell wall

6. The graph shows the effect of light intensity on the rate of photosynthesis at two different temperatures. The concentration of carbon dioxide was kept constant at 0.05%.

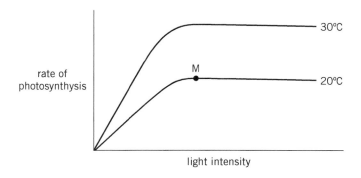

    State which factor is limiting the rate of photosynthesis at point M.

    A the concentration of carbon dioxide

    B light intensity

    C temperature

    D availability of chlorophyll

7. State which of the following is **not** the result of negative feedback.

    A a decrease in blood glucose concentration leads to an increase in insulin secretion

    B an increase in blood glucose concentration leads to an increase in insulin secretion

    C a decrease in blood glucose concentration leads to a decrease in insulin secretion

    D an increase in blood glucose concentration leads to an increase in glucagon secretion

8. In a typical reflex action, the relay neurones

    A pass impulses from sensory neurones to motor neurones

    B pass impulses from receptors to motor neurones

    C pass impulses from effectors to motor neurones

    D pass impulses from sensory neurones to effectors

9. A fish has a single circulatory system. State which type of blood leaves the heart of a fish.

    A oxygenated blood at high pressure

    B deoxygenated blood at high pressure

    C oxygenated blood at low pressure

    D deoxygenated blood at low pressure

10.

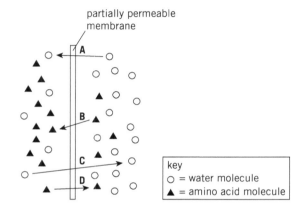

State which arrow

i. represents osmosis .... [1]

ii. represents active transport .... [1]

iii. represents diffusion of amino acids .... [1]

Longer written answers

Remember that there are also two alternative written papers. Paper 3 contains questions that only assess material from the **core** syllabus, paper 4 contains questions that could contain material from either the **core** or the **supplement**.

Sample 'core' questions

11. The diagram below shows the human alimentary canal.

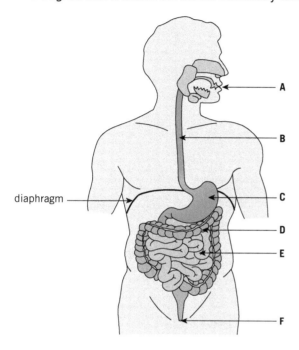

a. On the diagram, draw the liver in the correct place and approximately the right size. [2]

b. State the name of the process that moves food along the gut.

.... [1]

c. Use the diagram to complete the following table.

Each letter may be used once, more than once or not at all.

Description of site	Letter
Where saliva is released	
Where food is chewed	
Where hydrochloric acid is produced	
Where soluble foods are absorbed	
Where faeces are egested	

[5]

12. The diagram below shows how carbon may be recycled.

The letters represent processes that occur in the cycle.

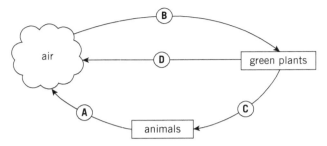

a. i. Use words from the following list to identify the processes **A, B, C,** and **D**.

feeding   photosynthesis   respiration

The words may be used once, more than once, or not at all.

Letter	Process
A	
B	
C	
D	

[4]

ii. Name and describe **one** other process which is part of a complete carbon cycle.

....

....

....

.... [3]

b. The diagram below shows a compost heap and the materials used to make it.

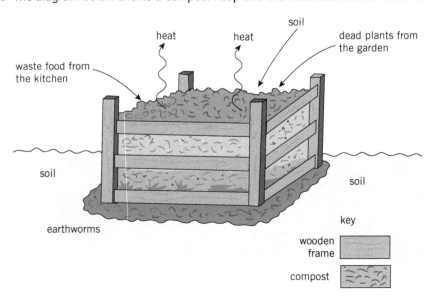

i. Explain why there is a difference in the temperature between the compost heap and the air surrounding it.

....

....

.... [2]

ii. Suggest one reason why a gardener uses an open frame to support the compost heap, rather than closed sides of the frame.

.... [1]

13. The diagram below shows a section through an air sac and a surrounding blood capillary.

   a. i. List three features shown in the diagram that make an air sac an efficient site for the exchange of gases.

   1. ....

   2. ....

   3. .... [3]

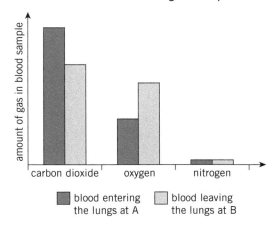

   ii. Suggest why the walls of the air sac contain elastic fibres.

   .... [1]

   b. Use the bar graph to identify **two** differences between the composition of the blood at **A** compared with the composition of the blood at **B**.

   A and **B** are shown in the diagram for part **a**.

1. ....

....

2. ....

.... [2]

c. Suggest **three** ways in which smoking can reduce the efficiency of the lungs.

1. ....

....

2. ....

....

3. ....

.... [3]

14. *In vitro* fertilisation may be helpful to couples who cannot conceive naturally.

This diagram shows the steps in this process

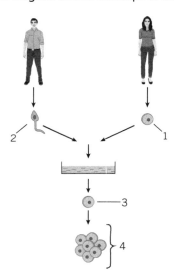

a. Match the structures A, B, C and D with the numbers 1–4 on the diagram

Letter A – D	Structure	Number 1 - 4
A	Fertilised egg	
B	Embryo	
C	Sperm	
D	Egg	

[3]

b. State the name of the type of cell division responsible for

    i. production of structure 2 .... [1]

    ii. production of structure 4 .... [1]

c. An embryo eventually differentiates into many different types of cell, forming tissues, organs and organ systems in an organism.

    i. State the name of the type of cell **in an adult** which retains the power to differentiate into several different tissues

    .... [1]

    ii. Suggest one site where this type of cell might be found in an adult human

    .... [1]

15. Phenyketonuria is an inherited disease. The allele for the disease (p) is recessive to the normal allele (P). The diagram below shows the inheritance of PKU in three generations of one family.

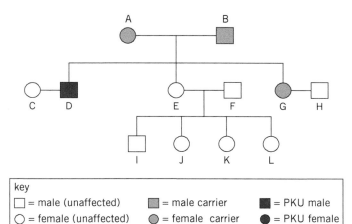

key
☐ = male (unaffected)   ▨ = male carrier   ■ = PKU male
○ = female (unaffected)   ◑ = female carrier   ● = PKU female

a. Write down the genotype of the individuals G and K

    G ....   K .... [2]

b. State how many of the children of the couple A and B are homozygous .... [1]

c. If C and D have a child, what is the probability that the child will have PKU?

    .... [1]

d. E and F have four children. All are male. What is the probability that their next child will be male?

    .... [1]

Sample 'supplement' questions

16. The diagram shows apparatus used to investigate the action of yeast on glucose solution.

    In Experiment **A**, 3 g of yeast were added to 10% glucose solution which had previously been boiled and cooled to 30 °C. The mixture was then placed into a vacuum flask.

    The procedure was repeated for Experiment **B** except the temperature was reduced to 20°C.

    The time taken for the hydrogencarbonate indicator to turn from orange-red to yellow was measured and noted.

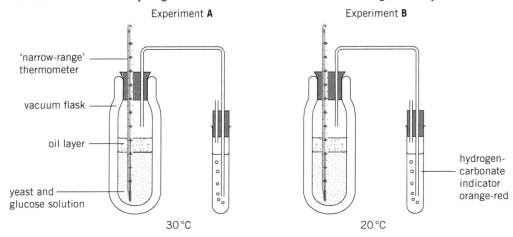

The results of the investigation are shown in this table.

	Experiment **A**	Experiment **B**
Temperature at start of experiment / °C	30.0	20.0
Temperature 3 hours later / °C	31.2	20.5
Time taken for indicator to change colour / min	58	93

a. Explain why the time taken for the indicator to change colour was different in experiments **A** and **B**.

....

.... [2]

b. i. Suggest why a layer of oil was placed on the surface of the solutions in flasks **A** and **B**.

.... [1]

ii. Explain why the 10% glucose solution was boiled before it was cooled and mixed with the yeast.

.... [1]

c. Write a chemical equation to describe the living process which is occurring inside the two flasks.

[2]

17. a. The following sentences describe the feeding relationships between four organisms.

    Owls obtain some of their energy from thrushes

    Apple moth caterpillars are herbivores

    An apple tree carries out photosynthesis

    Thrushes are secondary consumers

i. Write out a food chain containing these four organisms.

[3]

ii. State the main source of energy for the food chain

.... [1]

b. A group of students studied all of the organisms in an orchard of apple trees. They estimated the biomass of the different organisms.

The students divided the organisms into four groups according to their positions in the food web. Their results are shown in the table. Detritivores are animals that feed on parts of dead organisms.

Position of organisms in the food web	Biomass / g per m² of orchard
Producers	280
Herbivores	105
Detritivores	90
Carnivores	25

i. Use the information in the table to complete a pyramid of biomass on the grid. The scientists observed the detritivores feeding on dead plants, so decided to count herbivores and detritivores as one group of organisms.

(subdivide sectors into tens on grid)

ii. Define the term **trophic level**. ....

.... [1]

iii. Explain why there are very rarely more than four or five trophic levels in an ecosystem.

....

....

.... [2]

iv. The scientists obtained records of animal numbers over a period of years. They noticed that the number of owls was falling, and classified the owls as 'endangered'.

A species becomes endangered when it is at danger of extinction.

Suggest **two** ways in which an animal could become endangered.

....

....

.... [2]

Suggest **one** way in which endangered species can be conserved. ....

....

.... [2]

18. A doctor asked a patient to look carefully at the food labels of each item she ate during one day, and to note down

    i.   the different foods she ate

    ii. the salt content of each food

    iii. what proportion of the recommended daily amount (RDA) of salt to which this was equivalent.

    a. Suggest why too much salt in the diet can be harmful. ....

    .... [1]

    b. The results she obtained are shown in this table

Food	Amount of salt in food / g	% of RDA of salt
Breakfast cereal	0.2	3.3
Toast and butter	0.9	15.0
Tinned pasta	2.0	33.0
Tin of vegetable soup	2.5	41.7
Tinned beans	0.7	11.7
Ketchup	0.5	8.2
Chicken pie	1.3	21.7

    i. State the range for the amount of salt in the different foods. ....[2]

    ii. The RDA for salt is 6.0 g. Calculate how much more than the RDA of salt the patient ate.

    .... [2]

    c. As well as salt, some other foods are essential in small quantities. Suggest which of the foods in the above list would provide most vitamin D.

    .... [1]

Absorption: Movement of small food molecules and ions through the wall of the intestine into the blood or lymph.

Accommodation: The adjustment of the shape of the lens to accurately focus light onto the retina.

Active immunity: Defence against a pathogen, or response to a vaccine, by antibody production in the body.

Active transport: The movement of particles from a region of lower concentration to one of higher concentration, across a membrane, using energy from respiration.

Adaptive feature: An inherited feature that helps an organism to survive and reproduce in its environment.

Adrenaline: Hormone produced by the adrenal glands and prepares the body for stress – the 'fright, flight or fight' hormone.

Aerobic respiration: The chemical reactions in cells that use oxygen to break down food molecules and release a relatively large amount of energy.

AIDS: The weakening of the body's immune system, following infection by HIV.

Allele: An alternative form of a gene (a gene may have two or more alleles).

Amino acid: A sub-unit of a protein.

Amylase: The enzyme that digests starch to maltose.

Anaerobic respiration: The chemical reactions in cells that break down food molecules in the absence of oxygen and release a relatively small amount of energy.

Anaemia: An inability of the red blood cells to carry oxygen. Caused by faulty haemoglobin, and leads to weakness.

Anther: A male part of a flower, where pollen grains are produced.

Antibiotic: A drug (penicillin, for example) which slows the growth of, or kills, bacteria in the body.

Antibody: A protein released by lymphocytes which can recognise and bind to antigens.

Antigen: A molecule, often part of a pathogen, which can be recognised by the immune system.

Antiseptic: A substance which kills bacteria outside the body, on a kitchen surface for example.

Artery: A blood vessel which carries blood away from the heart.

Arthropod: An animal with jointed legs and a hard exoskeleton.

Artificial insemination(AI): Placing semen into the uterus as means of increasing fertility.

Artificial selection: The choice of animals or plants for breeding because they have characteristics useful to humans e.g. a high yield of milk.

Asexual reproduction: Reproduction without the involvement of gametes or zygotes so that offspring are genetically identical to their parents.

Assimilation: The use of digested food molecules by cells e.g. the synthesis of proteins from amino acids.

Atrium: A chamber of the heart that receives blood from veins and pumps it through to a ventricle.

Auxin: A plant growth hormone which is involved in tropic responses as it controls cell elongation.

Bacterium: Microorganism with cells that have cytoplasm and a cell wall, but no distinct nucleus. A prokaryote.

Balanced diet: A diet that provides carbohydrates, fats, proteins, vitamins, minerals, water and fibre in the correct proportions.

Bile: An alkaline fluid made in the liver and stored in the gall bladder. Bile is important in emulsification of fats in the small intestine and in the creation of an alkaline pH for the action of digestive enzymes there.

Binary fission: Asexual reproduction in which one cell divides into two, then two into four and so on.

Binomial system: Naming species in a system in which the scientific name of an organism is made up of two parts, showing the genus and the species. Humans, for example, have the binomial name *Homo sapiens*.

Biodegradable: Material that can be broken down by biological processes, usually involving microorganisms.

Biodiversity: The number and variety of living organisms.

Biomass: The mass of material, in a given area, derived from living organisms.

Biotechnology: The use of living organisms to carry out processes useful to humans, such as producing medicines or degrading wastes.

Blind spot: Part of the retina where the optic nerve leaves the eyeball so there are no photoreceptors.

Capillary: The smallest blood vessel, joining arteries to veins. The capillary is the site of exchange between blood and tissue fluid and has walls only one cell thick.

Cancer: Uncontrolled cell division leading to disease.

Carbohydrate: A class of molecule, containing carbon, hydrogen, and oxygen, and a major source of energy in food. Examples are starch and glucose.

Carnivore: An animal that gets its energy and raw materials by eating other animals.

Carrier: In genetics, an individual heterozygous for a recessive allele. The allele is not expressed but can be 'carried' to the next generation.

Catalyst: A substance that increases the rate of a chemical reaction and is not changed by the reaction.

Cellulose: An insoluble carbohydrate that makes up the cell wall of plant cells.

Central nervous system (CNS): The brain and spinal cord.

Chemical digestion: Breakdown of large, insoluble food molecules into small soluble ones. The process usually involves enzymes.

Chlorophyll: The green pigment, found within the chloroplast of plant cells, which absorbs light energy for photosynthesis.

Chloroplast: Organelle in plant cells that contains chlorophyll and carries out photosynthesis.

Cholera: A disease of the intestines in which water reabsorption is affected. Caused by a bacterium, *Vibrio cholerae*.

Cholesterol: A lipid-like molecule which is linked to higher risks of atherosclerosis and heart disease.

Chromosome: A thread-like structure of DNA, carrying genetic information in the form of genes.

Clone: A group of genetically identical organisms. Usually formed by mitosis.

Clotting: A series of processes that cause blood cells and fragments to clump together and seal damaged blood vessels.

Codominance: The existence of two alleles of a gene where neither is dominant over the other, and both are expressed in the heterozygote. The alleles I^A and I^B for blood groups are an example.

Community: All of the populations of different species in an ecosystem.

Competition: The situation in which different organisms are seeking the same resource, such as food or nesting sites.

Concentration gradient: The difference in concentration of a solute between two different places.

Conservation: Work carried out by humans to protect species and maintain biodiversity, or to maintain a supply of limited resources.

Consumer: An organism that gets its energy by feeding on other organisms.

Continuous variation: Differences between organisms that show a range of phenotypes between extremes with many intermediates. Often results from effects of both genes and the environment.

Coronary heart disease (CHD): Disease of the heart caused by blockage of the coronary arteries. Risk is increased by fatty diets and poor exercise habits.

Cross pollination: Transfer of pollen grains from the anther of one flower to the stigma on a different plant of the same species.

Cystic fibrosis: Disease of the lungs and digestive system caused by excessive secretion of sticky mucus. Results from a mutant recessive allele so is only expressed in homozygous individuals.

Deamination: The removal of the nitrogen-containing part of amino acids to form urea.

Decomposer: An organism that gets its energy from dead or waste organic material.

Deforestation: The removal of trees by humans to clear land for agriculture or for building.

Denitrification: Conversion of nitrate to nitrogen by bacteria, as part of the nitrogen cycle.

Development: The increase in complexity of an organism as it grows and produces new tissues, organs, and systems.

Diabetes: A medical condition in which the blood glucose concentration is not controlled. Can be caused by failure of the pancreas to secrete insulin or by a diet high in sugars.

DCPIP: A chemical which can be used to measure the concentration of vitamin C in a solution, as it is decolourised from blue to colourless.

Diffusion: The net movement of particles from a region of higher concentration to one of lower concentration. The particles move down a concentration gradient as their kinetic energy results in their random movement.

Digestion: The breakdown of large, insoluble molecules into smaller, soluble molecules using chemical and mechanical processes.

Diploid nucleus: A nucleus containing two sets of chromosomes, usually in pairs. Present in most body cells.

Discontinuous variation: Few phenotypes for a particular characteristic, with no intermediate forms. Typically the result of genes alone.

DNA: The molecule that forms the genetic material. Genetic information is stored as a sequence of bases in the DNA.

Dominant: An allele that is expressed if it is present in a heterozygote.

Drug: Any substance taken into the body that modifies or affects chemical reactions in the body.

Ecosystem: A unit containing the community of living organisms interacting with their physical environment.

Egestion: The passing out of food that has not been digested or absorbed, as faeces through the anus.

Embryo: The early stage of a plant or animal as it grows and develops by mitosis from a fertilised egg.

Emphysema: A lung disease in which the walls of the air sacs are broken down and so lose their ability to transfer oxygen and carbon dioxide between blood and air.

Emulsification: The breakdown of large fat globules into many smaller ones, in the presence of bile.

Enzymes: Proteins that function as biological catalysts.

Eutrophication: The effect of nitrates and phosphates on the growth of algae and aquatic plants. Can lead to a decrease in the oxygen content of water, and death of aerobic organisms.

Evolution: The process in which inherited features of organisms change over a period of time.

Excretion: Removal of toxic materials, waste products of metabolism and substances in excess of the body's requirements.

Extinction: The loss of a species from the Earth's community.

Fats: Lipids that are insoluble in water and contain three fatty acids linked to a glycerol molecule. Important as energy stores and in thermal insulation.

Fermentation: A form of anaerobic respiration in which glucose is converted to carbon dioxide and alcohol. The term is also used to describe industrial processes in which microorganisms make products useful to humans.

Fermenter: A large container where microorganisms can be grown under controlled conditions to make useful products. Also called a bioreactor.

Fertilisation: The fusion of male and female gametes to produce a zygote.

Fertiliser: Plant nutrients that can be used to stimulate plant growth. Usually contain nitrate, phosphate, and, often, potassium.

Fetus: A stage during the development of a mammal when all the major organs are present.

Fibre: Indigestible plant material that helps the action of the alimentary canal and the formation of faeces.

Food chain: The transfer of energy from one organism to the next, beginning with the absorption of light energy by a producer.

Food web: A network of interconnected food chains.

Gall bladder: A sac in the liver which stores bile before its release into the small intestine.

Gametes: Sex cells with the haploid number of chromosomes e.g. sperm and egg in animals.

Gene: A length of DNA that codes for a protein.

Gene mutation: A change in the base sequence of DNA.

Genetic engineering: Changing the genetic material of an organism by removing, changing or inserting individual genes.

Genotype: The genetic make-up of an organism in terms of the genes present.

Genus: A unit of classification containing a group of species with similar characteristics.

Glucagon: Hormone produced by the pancreas that helps to increase blood glucose concentration by stimulating the liver to convert glycogen to glucose.

Glycogen: An insoluble carbohydrate used as an energy store in animal cells, usually in the liver and muscles.

Gravtitropism: A response in which parts of a plant grow towards (positive) or away from (negative) gravity.

Greenhouse effect: Keeping the Earth's surface warm as greenhouse gases, especially carbon dioxide and methane, reduce the loss of heat energy through the atmosphere. Occurs naturally but is becoming more extreme (enhanced) by emissions resulting from human activity.

Growth: A permanent increase in size and dry mass by an increase in cell size and/or cell number.

Haemoglobin: The red pigment in red blood cells. Contains iron, and combines with oxygen so that the red cells can carry this gas.

Haploid nucleus: A nucleus containing a single set of unpaired chromosomes e.g. in gametes.

Herbivore: An animal that obtains its energy and raw materials by eating plants.

Heterozygous: Having two different alleles of a particular gene.

HIV (Human Immunodeficiency Virus): The virus that attacks lymphocytes and so reduces the efficiency of the human immune system, leading to AIDS.

Homeostasis: The maintenance of a constant internal environment.

Homologous chromosomes: A pair of matching chromosomes that carry genes for the same characteristic in the same positions.

Homozygous: Having two identical alleles of a particular gene.

Hormone: A chemical substance produced by a gland and carried in the blood and alters the activity of one or more specific target organs.

Immunity: Protection against infection by pathogens using antibodies and cells such as phagocytes.

Implantation: The embedding of an embryo into the wall of the uterus at the start of the gestation period in mammals.

Ingestion: The taking in of substances into the body through the mouth.

Inheritance: The transmission of genetic information from generation to generation.

Insulin: Hormone secreted by the pancreas which reduces the blood glucose concentration.

***In vitro* fertilisation (IVF):** The mixing of sperm and eggs in a dish outside the body. The gametes fuse at fertilisation and the resulting embryo is inserted into the uterus.

Iris: A ring of muscle which controls the entry of light into the eye and so can protect the retina from over-stimulation.

Lactase: Enzyme which breaks down milk sugar (lactose). Can be immobilised for use in the preparation of lactose-free milk.

Lacteal: Structure inside the villus which transports absorbed fats away from the intestine.

Lactic acid: A product of anaerobic respiration in animals.

Lens: A structure responsible for the fine focussing of light on the retina.

Limiting factor: Something present in the environment in such short supply that it restricts life processes e.g. light intensity may be the limiting factor that limits the rate of photosynthesis.

Ligase: An enzyme used in genetic engineering used to stitch together two pieces of DNA, such as a plasmid and an opened chromosome.

Lipase: Enzyme which digests fats to fatty acids and glycerol.

Liver: Organ which carries out many of the reactions of metabolism, including production of bile and deamination of excess amino acids.

Malnutrition: Condition caused by eating an unbalanced diet. Can be undernutrition when the diet is deficient in some way, or overnutrition when some part of the diet is present in excess.

Mechanical digestion: The physical breakdown of food into smaller pieces, without the involvement of enzymes e.g. by chewing with teeth.

Meiosis: Division of the nucleus to produce cells (gametes) with half of the normal chromosome number. The gametes also contain different combinations of genetic material.

Memory cells: Cells produced as a result of exposure to an antigen, for example in a vaccine, so that the body is prepared for further infection by the same antigen.

Menstruation: The breakdown of the lining of the uterus as part of the menstrual cycle so that blood and cells are discharged through the vagina.

Metabolism: The sum of the chemical reactions occurring in cells.

Mitochondrion: Organelle which carries out aerobic respiration and so provides energy for metabolism.

Mitosis: Division of the nucleus which produces genetically identical cells with the same chromosome number as the parent cells.

Motor neurone: Nerve cell which carries impulses from the CNS to an effector such as a muscle.

Movement: An action causing a change in position of an organism or part of an organism.

Mutation: A change in the genetic material of an organism. Occurs naturally but rate can be increased by radiation or by some chemicals.

Natural selection: The effect of the environment on the survival of individuals so that different individuals are able to pass on their genetic material to successive generations.

Negative feedback: The mechanism for maintaining homeostasis in which a change from the optimum conditions causes a response to cancel out the change.

Nitrification: Conversion of ammonium ions to nitrate, as part of the nitrogen cycle.

Nitrogen fixation: Conversion of nitrogen gas to nitrogen-containing compounds. Often carried out by bacteria in nodules on the roots of legumes.

Nucleus: Control centre of the cell, contains the chromosomes.

Nutrition: The taking in of materials for energy, growth, and development.

Obesity: A body mass which is greater than that recommended for good health. May be caused by overnutrition, where energy consumed is greatly in excess of energy needs.

Oestrogen: Hormone responsible for development of female secondary sexual characteristics.

Organ: A structure made of a group of different tissues working together to perform a specific function.

Organ system: A group of organs working together to perform a specific function in the body e.g. stomach, ileum, colon, and rectum in the digestive system.

Osmosis: The net movement of water molecules from a region of higher water potential to one of lower water potential, through a partially permeable membrane.

Ovule: The structure inside the ovary of a plant that contains the female gamete. After fertilisation the ovule develops into a seed.

Ovum: Female sex cell (gamete), produced in the ovary.

Oxygen debt: The extra oxygen 'owed' to the body to respire lactic acid produced during anaerobic respiration in animals.

Pancreas: The organ which (a) produces insulin and glucagon to regulate blood glucose concentration and (b) produces digestive enzymes active in the small intestine.

Partially permeable membrane: A membrane, such as the cell membrane, that allows some particles to pass through but prevents the passage of others. Sometimes called a selectively permeable membrane.

Passive immunity: Short-term defence against a pathogen by antibodies provided by another individual e.g. from mother to infant in breast milk.

Pathogen: A disease-causing organism.

Pectinase: An enzyme that breaks down plant cell walls and can be used for 'clearing' fruit juices.

Pesticide: A chemical that kills pests (a pest is an organism that competes with humans for resources).

Phagocyte: A type of white blood cell that ingests and digest pathogens as part of an immune response.

Phenotype: The observable features of an organism; affected by both genes and environment.

Phloem: Plant tissue which transports the products of photosynthesis such as sucrose.

Photosynthesis: The process by which plants manufacture carbohydrates from carbon dioxide and water, using energy from light.

Phototropism: A response in which parts of a plant grow towards (positive) or away from (negative) the direction from which light is coming.

Plasma: The liquid part of blood, responsible for transporting many solutes such as dissolved foods, urea and hormones.

Plasmid: A small ring of DNA found in bacterial cells and useful as a vector in genetic engineering.

Platelets: Small fragments of red blood cells used in the blood clotting process.

Pollination: Transfer of pollen grains from anther to stigma, of the same or a different plant.

Population: A group of organisms of a single species living in the same area at the same time.

Producer: An organism that makes its own organic nutrients, usually using energy from sunlight, by photosynthesis.

Prokaryote: A cell without its DNA contained inside a clear nucleus.

Protease: Enzyme which digests protein to amino acids.

Protein: Large molecule composed of amino acids linked by peptide bonds.

Protoctist: Microscopic single-celled organism which may have some animal features (e.g. *Amoeba*) or some plant features (e.g. *Euglena*).

Puberty: The stage of development at which secondary sexual characteristics appear.

Pulse: An expansion of the elastic wall of an artery as blood is forced out from the left ventricle of the heart.

Pyramid of biomass: An illustration of the amount of biomass at each trophic level in an ecosystem.

Pyramid of numbers: An illustration of the number of organisms at each trophic level in an ecosystem.

Receptor: Cell which can receive a stimulus and then produce an impulse.

Recessive: One of a pair of alleles that is only expressed when in the homozygous condition.

Recycling: Conversion of waste material back to a form in which it can be useful to humans.

Red blood cell: Cell which transports oxygen from lung to tissues.

Reflex action: An automatic response to a given stimulus, which often has a survival value.

Relay neurone: A nerve cell within the CNS which transfers impulses from a sensory neurone to a motor neurone.

Reproduction: The process that make more of the same kind of organism.

Respiration: The chemical processes in the cell that break down nutrient molecules to release energy for metabolism.

Response: An action carried out by an effector as a result of a particular stimulus.

Restriction enzyme: An enzyme used in genetic engineering to cut DNA at specific places.

Retina: The light-sensitive layer of the eye, containing the photoreceptors rods and cones.

Ribosome: Organelle which can synthesise proteins from amino acids.

Root hair: Specialised cell in a root that provides a large surface area for the absorption of water and mineral ions.

Rough endoplasmic reticulum: A network of membranes inside cells with ribosomes attached for the efficient synthesis of proteins from amino acids.

Secretion: The release of a useful product from a cell e.g. mucus from goblet cells in the bronchi.

Selective breeding: The choice of animals or plants for breeding because they have characteristics useful to humans e.g. a high yield of milk.

Self pollination: The transfer of pollen from the anther to the stigma of the same flower.

Sense organ: A collection of receptor cells sensitive to the same stimulus e.g. the eye is a sense organ sensitive to light.

Sensitivity: The ability to detect and respond to changes in the environment.

Sensory neurone: Nerve cell which carries impulses from a receptor to the CNS.

Sex chromosomes: A pair of chromosomes which determine the sex of an individual e.g. in humans XX is female and XY is male.

Sex-linked characteristic: A characteristic for which the gene responsible is located on a sex chromosome, usually the X chromosome.

Sexual reproduction: A process involving the fusion of the nuclei of two gametes (sex cells) to form a zygote, and the formation of offspring that are genetically different from one another and from their parents.

Sexually transmitted infection (STI): An infection that is transmitted in body fluids through sexual contact.

Species: A group of animals with so many similar characteristics that they are capable of interbreeding and producing fertile offspring.

Sperm: Male sex cell (gamete) produced in the testes.

Starch: An insoluble carbohydrate often used as an energy store in plant cells.

Stem cells: Unspecialised cells that multiply by mitosis and then can become specialised to form a range of different tissues e.g. cells in the bone marrow can become different types of blood cell.

Stimulus: A change in the environment that can be detected by a receptor.

Stoma (plural: stomata): A small gap in the epidermis of a leaf that allows gases to diffuse in and out. The size of the gap is controlled by guard cells.

Sustainable development: Development providing resources for an increasing human population without changing the environment to make it unsuitable for future generations.

Sustainable resource: One that is produced as rapidly as it is removed from the environment so that it does not run out e.g. timber from managed forests.

Synapse: A junction between two neurones.

Test cross: A genetic cross which crosses a known genotype (a homozygous recessive) with another organism in order to work out the unknown genotype.

Testosterone: Male sex hormone, produced in the testes, responsible for the development of male secondary sexual characteristics.

Tissue: A group of cells with similar structures working together to carry out a particular function

Translocation: The movement of the products of photosynthesis, sucrose and amino acids, through the phloem.

Transmissible disease: A disease in which the pathogen can be passed from one host to another.

Transpiration: Loss of water by plant leaves by evaporation and diffusion.

Trophic level: The position of an organism in a food chain, food web, pyramid of numbers or pyramid of biomass.

Tropism: A growth response of part of a plant to an external stimulus, such as light or gravity.

Turgor: A pressure inside a plant cell caused by the cytoplasm pushing against the cellulose cell wall.

Urea: A waste product produced by deamination of amino acids in the liver. It is expelled from the blood as urine from the kidneys.

Urine: An excretory fluid formed in the kidneys by filtration of the blood. It contains urea, salts, and variable amounts of water.

Uterus: A muscular chamber in the female where an implanted embryo develops into a fetus during the gestation period. Also known as the womb.

Vaccine: A product containing a mild or killed pathogen to stimulate the activity of the immune system and so provide protection against a disease.

Vaccination: The process of delivering a vaccine to provide immunity.

Vacuole: A fluid-filled sac present in most plant cells but very rarely in animal cells.

Vagina: A muscular tube leading from the uterus to the outside which acts as the birth canal.

Variation: Differences between individuals of the same species – may be continuous or discontinuous.

Vasoconstriction: Reduction in the diameter of blood vessels, especially in the skin when conserving heat.

Vasodilation: Increase in the diameter of blood vessels, especially in the skin when trying to lose heat.

Vein: Blood vessel which returns blood towards the heart, often with the help of flap-like valves.

Ventricle: Lower chamber of the heart, which is muscular to expel blood into the arteries.

Vertebrate: An animal with a backbone.

Villus: A structure which increases the surface area of the small intestine to increase the surface area for absorption of digested food molecules.

Virus: A microscopic organism, containing nucleic acid surrounded by a protein coat, and which can only reproduce inside a living cell.

Vitamin: A nutrient needed in very small amounts but which is essential to aid the use of other nutrients.

Water potential: The tendency for water molecules to move by diffusion i.e. down a gradient of water potential.

White blood cells: Cells which are usually involved with defence against disease or infection. Includes lymphocytes and phagocytes.

Wilting: Drooping of plants as water loss causes a loss of turgor in the plant cells.

Xerophyte: A plant adapted to life in very dry environments.

Xylem: The tissue in a plant through which water and minerals are transported.

Yeast: A single-celled fungus that is widely used in biotechnology as it converts glucose to alcohol and carbon dioxide.

Zygote: The product of fertilisation i.e. the fusion of male and female gametes.

Unit 1.1
1. A: sensitivity; B: reproduction; C: excretion; D: respiration
2. C
3. kingdom – phylum – class – order – family – genus – species

Unit 1.2
1. a. *Parus caeruleus* and *Parus major;* they belong to the same genus
   b. i.
E. rubecula	✗	✗	✗
P. caeruleus	✗	✓	✓
P. major	✗	✓	✓
T. merula	✓	✗	✗
   ii. Pale area only below eye *Parus major*
   Pale areas above and below eye *Parus caeruleus*

Unit 1.3
1. a. i. chloroplast ii. nutrition (photosynthesis)
   b. i. excretion ii. movement
   c. respiration

Unit 1.4
1. a. stem – hold leaves in best position; root – absorb water and mineral ions; leaves – trap light energy for photosynthesis; flowers – may be attractive to pollinating insects or birds; fruit – usually help dispersal of seed, a reproductive structure
   b. chlorophyll; autotrophic; photosynthesis; cellulose; ferns angiosperms; monocotyledons; dicotyledons

Unit 1.5
1. a. ant: three/yes; earthworm: none/no; centipede: many/yes; mite: four/no
   b. ant – insect; earthworm – annelid; centipede – myriapod; mite – arachnid

Unit 1.6
1. a. An animal with a backbone
   b. scales; no; no; yes; fur; yes

Unit 2.1
1. a. phloem – transport; stamens – reproductive
   b. i. Could label nucleus/cell membrane/cytoplasm
   ii. chloroplast
   iii. cellulose cell wall/permanent vacuole
   c. i. mitochondrion/mitochondria
   ii. ribosomes (accept rough endoplasmic reticulum)

Unit 2.2
1. a. 10
   b. 1000
2. a. A – cell surface membrane; B – cytoplasm; C – nucleus
   b. nucleus
   c. cellulose cell wall/chloroplast/permanent vacuole
   d. 3 cm = 30 000 µm; Magnification = $\frac{30\,000}{25}$ = ×1200

Unit 2.3
1. a. From top line, reading right to left: cell C, 1, 2, 3; cell B, 1, 2, 3; cell F, 1, 4, 5, 6, 7; cell I, 1, 4, 5, 8; cell E, 1, 4, 5, 6; cell A, 1, 2; cell H, 1, 4, 5, 8; cell D, 1, 4; cell G , 1, 4, 5, 6, 7
   b. leaf

Unit 2.4
Across:
2. chlorophyll
3. human
4. arthropods
6. photosynthesis
8. fish
9. invertebrates
11. vertebrates
13. amphibian
16. reptile
17. kingdoms
20. insects
22. legs
23. spiders
24. fungi
Down:
1. feathers
2. classification
5. conifer
7. key
10. bird
12. mammals
14. protist
15. species
18. moss
19. fern
21. wings

Unit 3.1
1. a. Diffusion; down; gas; random; equilibrium; Osmosis; diffusion; potential; partially permeable
2. Na⁺ ion – active transport; K⁺ ion – diffusion; water – osmosis

Unit 3.2
1. a. i. +8, +4, −1, −6, −10
   ii. graph plotted
   iii. 0.45
   iv. Represents an equilibrium so shows water potential of cell cytoplasm
   b. osmosis

Unit 3.3
1. a. i. B
   ii. C
   b. D
   c. Movement is against a concentration gradient
   d. 1. Mineral ion, e.g. magnesium ion into root hair
   2. Glucose/amino acids from gut contents across villi into bloodstream

Unit 4.1
1. a. glucose; cellulose; sucrose; soluble
   b. fatty acids; glycerol; insoluble
   c. haemoglobin; amino acids; soluble
   d. DNA
2. a. i. vitamin C ii. blue to colourless
   b. orange juice

Unit 4.2
1. a. i. higher protein content
   ii. Earlier step in food chain, so more can be produced per unit area.
   b. i. sample Z
   ii. as a reagent blank
   iii. sample X

Unit 4.3
1. a. calcium – Involved in bone and tooth structure; iron – A part of the haemoglobin molecule; Vitamin C – Helps in formation of collagen fibres; Vitamin D – Required for the absorption of calcium; phospholipid – Forms the main part of cell membranes
   b. i. pure fruit juice – 2.20; stored fruit juice – 3.30; heated fruit juice – 3.25
   ii. storage has more effect
   iii. increase in body mass may lead to obesity; sugar may cause tooth decay

Unit 4.4
1. a. i. brain ii. fat
   b. Good solvent – carries dissolved substances in blood plasma
   Transparent – allows photosynthesis underwater
   High heat capacity – helps to keep a constant body temperature
   High latent heat of evaporation – aids heat loss via sweating
   Solid ice less dense than liquid water – ice floats and so provides a habitat for penguins

Answers

Unit 5.4

1. Protein – the type of molecule that makes up an enzyme; substrate – a molecule that reacts in an enzyme-catalysed reaction; product – the molecule made in an enzyme-catalysed reaction; active site – the part of the enzyme where substrate molecules can bind; denaturation – a change in shape of an enzyme so that its active site cannot bind to the substrate; optimum – the ideal value of a factor, such as temperature, for an enzyme to work
2. Lipase; cuts out useful genes from chromosomes; removes milk sugar from milk; protease; cellulase; amylase

Unit 5.5

1. a. Check correct column headings, e.g. temperature °C and time for clotting/minutes
    b. Graph plotted – temperature on x axis
    c. 45°C
    d. i. pH
       ii. Use buffer solutions

Unit 5.6

1. a. i. amino acids/peptides
       ii. 54 mg
    b. i. 7.0/8.0
       ii. 2.4
    c. Hydrochloric acid is added from cells lining the glands of the stomach
    d. i. lipase
       ii. fatty acids and glycerol
       iii. Bile; by breaking it down to fat droplets (emulsification) increases surface area for action of lipase

Unit 5.7

1. a. temperature on x axis, time taken on y axis
    b. 35°C
    c. These are fixed variables.
    d. Enzyme is denatured – loss of active site so cannot have binding of substrate to enzyme
    e. pH/enzyme concentration/substrate concentration

Unit 6.1

1. photosynthesis; light/solar; chloroplasts/chlorophyll; carbon dioxide; water; starch; oxygen; stomata
2. a. carbon dioxide
    b. oxygen
    c. water
    d. nitrate
    e. magnesium

Unit 6.2

1. a. 3.5 arbitrary units
    b. Light intensity is the limiting factor up to 6 arbitrary units. At this point, some other factor (temperature, for example) is at a value which is preventing further photosynthesis.

Unit 6.3

1. a. A – upper epidermis; B – palisade mesophyll; C – spongy mesophyll; D – guard cell; E – xylem vessel
    b. B
    c. E
    d. sucrose
    e. i. 0.9 mm
       ii. 0.25 mm

Unit 6.4

1. a. i. carbon dioxide
       ii. oxygen
    b. diffusion
    c. i. This-stroy 19.5 g   ii. water 33 g
       ii. $32.9 - 19.2 = 13.7$ $\frac{13.7}{32.9} \times 100 = 41.6$
       iii. Measured 'dry' mass because 'water' content (and so wet mass) can greatly fluctuate.

Unit 6.5

1. a. Light intensity 10 arbitrary units, carbon dioxide concentration 0.15% at 30°C. Make sure that you give all of the units in your answer!
    b. Even at the same light intensity and temperature, increasing the carbon dioxide concentration from 0.04% to 0.15% increased the rate of photosynthesis by as much as 375%.
    c. Carbon dioxide concentration is the limiting factor under those sets of conditions.

Unit 6.6

1. a. To act as a control. In this case to show that the indicator does not change colour due to some other factor.
    b. To make sure that this is a fixed variable, i.e. volume of indicator should not affect the results.
    c. i. photosynthesis
       ii. respiration
       iii. respiration
    d. These plants require a high light intensity to photosynthesise, and light intensity would be low in the forest environment.

Unit 6.7

1. a. i. To allow measurement of the maximum (complete solution) and minimum (water) rate of growth of the wheat seedlings.
       ii. Air contains oxygen and oxygen is needed for aerobic respiration. This releases energy for active uptake of mineral ions by the root hair cells.
       iii. Magnesium is required to produce chlorophyll. No chlorophyll means very limited photosynthesis so very poor growth.
    b. nitrogen   phosphorus   potassium

Unit 7.2

1. a. 70% = 55% + 15% (each segment represents 5%)
    b. From the top of the list: T; F; T; F; T; T; F; T; F; F; T; F; F; T; F

Unit 7.3

1. a. y axis energy requirement (kJ/day × 1000), x axis type of person
    b. i. age – teenage boy needs more energy than eight-year-old; gender – male IT worker needs more energy than female IT worker; activity – manual worker needs more energy than IT worker
       ii. female is lighter than a male, so less mass to move about
       iii. Vitamin D: rickets (more likelihood of broken bones/night blindness). Iron: anaemia/tiredness, since less haemoglobin/red blood cells produced so less oxygen transported.

Unit 7.4

1. a. Carbohydrate and fat/lipid
    b. i. More
       ii. $\frac{2719}{9000} \times 100 = 30.2\%$
       iii. Jack is heavier/more active/growing more quickly

Unit 7.6

1. a. i. male
       ii. female, aged 20–24
    b. i. as fat
       ii. diabetes/arthritis/heart disease
    c. Provision of an unbalanced diet.
    d. i. vitamin D   ii. calcium
       iii. Lack of growth/replacement of enzymes

Unit 7.7

1. Salivary glands – produce an alkaline liquid which lubricates food making it easier to swallow; oesophagus – carries a bolus of food from mouth to stomach; stomach – produces hydrochloric acid and begins digestion of protein; Ileum – where most digested food is absorbed; pancreas – produces a set of enzymes which pass into the duodenum; gall bladder – stores bile produced in the liver; colon – where most of the water is reabsorbed from the contents of the intestine; rectum – stores waste food as faeces.
2. bread; butter; egg; mouth; molars; surface area; large; smaller; capillaries

Unit 7.8
1. a. i. A – dentine; B – cement; C – crown.
   ii. blood vessels/nerves
2. a. Using a pH meter on a sample of saliva collected (e.g. by chewing a rubber band).
   b. pH affects the number of fillings
   c. Hypothesis supported; the increased pH shows a reduction in the number of fillings.

Unit 7.9
1. a. With iodine solution: straw-brown; blue-black; blue-black; blue-black
      With Benedict's reagent: orange-red   blue   blue   blue
   b. mouth (from salivary glands), small intestine (from pancreas)
   c. This is the optimum temperature for amylase activity
   d. in the stomach

Unit 7.10
1. a. villus
   b. small intestine/ileum
   c. i. M – Should be linked to lacteal (at centre of villus)
      ii. N – should be linked to surface epithelium (produces mucus from goblet cells)
   d. large surface area increases rate of absorption, thin epithelium reduces distance for absorption; capillaries/lacteals remove absorbed products
   e. i. ×50
      ii. 1.5 mm

Unit 8.1
1. osmosis; hairs; surface area; ions; magnesium; diffusion; active transport; support; solvent; photosynthesis
2. a. reduces evaporation from leaf surface
   b. collect sample of leaves/weigh/allow to hang for 24 hours/reweigh/compare masses

Unit 8.2
1. a. A: phloem; B: xylem; C: epidermis
   b. i. B because this is xylem which transports water and water-soluble dyes such as eosin
      ii. Radioactive carbon dioxide is converted to radioactive carbohydrate by photosynthesis. The carbohydrate is transported, as sucrose, in the phloem. The phloem therefore shows up by fogging the photographic plate.

Unit 8.3
1. a. Mean mass at start = 220.4 g. Mean mass after 24 h = 210.2 g. Therefore mean loss of water = 220.4 − 210.2 = 10.2 g.
   b. Mean volume of water at start = 100 cm³ = 100 g. Mean volume of water after 24 h = 88 cm³ = 88 g. Therefore mean uptake of water = 12 g.
   c. Water uptake is driven by water loss from the stomata/leaves. Water lost 'pulls' a stream of water through the plant – this is replaced by water uptake at the roots.
   d. Some of the water absorbed by the roots is used for support or in photosynthesis, so the masses are not exactly the same.

Unit 8.4
1. a. D is incorrect
   b. Broad and fleshy leaves would mean much water loss in the dry desert environment.
2. a. Look for water vapour loss by diffusion through stomata, water evaporation from surface of spongy mesophyll cells.
   b. Windspeed/humidity of atmosphere/light intensity

Unit 9.1
1. a. i. pulmonary vein
      ii. A has less oxygen/more carbon dioxide/is at higher pressure
   b. E has more urea/more sodium/is at higher pressure
   c. Should be guideline to vessel just below chamber C

Unit 9.2
1. $5\,000\,000 = 5 \times 10^6$
2. a. Volume of blood = $5 \times 10^3 \times 10^3 = 5 \times 10^6$
   b. Therefore total number of RBC in circulation = $5 \times 10^6 \times 5 \times 10^6 = 25 \times 10^{12} = 2.5 \times 10^{13}$
   c. Number produced every day = $2.5 \times \dfrac{10^{13}}{10^2} = 2.5 \times 10^{11}$

Unit 9.3
1. a. i. left ventricle
      ii. thicker muscular walls
   b. pacemaker; 72
2. double
3. a. Blood pressure falls as blood passes through the gills, and cannot be raised again before blood reaches body tissues.
   b. kidneys
   c. Blood at low pressure can flow more easily through the wider veins.
   d. pulmonary arteries; tissue fluid/plasma

Unit 9.4
1. a. i. $100 - 45 = 55\%$
      ii. ions/glucose/amino acids/hormones
      iii. Red blood cell – transport of oxygen; phagocyte – engulfing invading microbes; lymphocyte – antibody production; platelet – part of clotting process
   b. Severe breathlessness/tiredness/inability to train hard
   c. They will have an increased number of red blood cells so their blood will be able to supply more oxygen than normal to the muscles, thus improving their performance.
   d. Testosterone (or some other steroid) – used because it increases growth of muscle tissue; anabolic steroid/muscle building; stimulants such as amphetamine/more powerful muscle contractions

Unit 9.5
1. a. Change the depth of heartbeat (stroke volume), i.e. volume of blood pumped with each heartbeat
   b. i. X - cuspid valve - pressure in ventricle exceeds pressure in atrium so valve closes to prevent backflow
      Y - semilunar valve closes, as pressure in left ventricle falls below pressure in aorta, to prevent backflow of blood into heart
      ii. in the veins
      iii. Maintain one-way flow of blood at lower pressure in the veins
   c. Blood flow to lungs is reduced so blood does not oxygenate well, and so blood (which shows up in the lips) is not as red as it normally would be.

Unit 9.6
1. a. i. From the top: 77, 72, 96, 81, 76, 102, 72, 89.
      ii. The boys appear to have a higher pulse rate.
   b. i. Exercise increases blood flow to heart, muscles, and skin, but reduces blood flow to gut and kidneys. Flow to brain does not change.
      ii. Blood delivers more oxygen and glucose for respiration needed to release the energy required for muscle contraction.
   c. i. Less oxygen is delivered to working heart muscle, so less energy is available and muscle stops working.
      ii. obesity/high fat consumption/high salt consumption

Unit 10.1
1. a. High temperature/vomiting/diarrhoea
   b. Not washing hands when preparing food for child/not using clean utensils and crockery/feeding with infected food
   c. Always wash hands when preparing food for child/cook food thoughly and at the correct temperature
2. Rickets/scurvy; cystic fibrosis/sickle cell anaemia; dementia/heart disease/cancer; lung cancer/CHD/diabetes type II

Unit 10.2
1. a. An organism capable of causing a disease.
   b. cholera bacterium – in infected water; influenza virus – in droplets in the air; athlete's foot fungus – by direct contact; plasmodium protoctist – by an insect vector; salmonella bacterium – in contaminated food; HIV – in infected body fluids

2. In infected body fluids; fungus; drying skin carefully; in infected water; bacterium; disposal of faeces correctly; bacterium; careful food preparation/cooking food thoroughly; virus; trapping sneezes and coughs in tissues or a handkerchief.

Unit 10.4

1. a. Food source column: fish; milk products; fresh meat; vegetables
Number of reported outbreaks column: 20; 45; 5
   b. At refrigeration temperatures, bacteria which might be present in the food cannot multiply, so cannot produce toxins which cause food poisoning.

Unit 10.5

1. a. A disease caused when cells divide/multiply out of control. The extra cells can cause damage directly or may use up nutrients from other 'normal' cells.
   b. i. breast cancer
      ii. $\frac{9}{100} \times 1000 = 90$
      iii. ovary, cervix, and uterus
   c. The disease can be identified before it causes too much damage. Treatment may destroy the cancer cells and so prolong life.

Unit 10.6

1. pathogen – a disease-causing organism; transmissible disease – condition in which the pathogen can be passed from one host to another; antigen – a substance which triggers the immune response; skin and nasal hairs – external barriers to infection; active immunity – defence against a pathogen by antibody production in the body; passive immunity – short-term defence by provision of antibodies from another individual; phagocyte – white blood cell that engulfs pathogens; lymphocyte – cell which produces antibodies
2. a. A chemical or cell which provokes the body's immune system to produce appropriate antibodies.
   b. Response is faster, greater, and lasts for longer.

Unit 10.7

1. B: a vaccine
2. a. Defence against a pathogen by the production of antibodies in the body.
   b. i. Antibodies are from another individual/the response does not last as long/no memory cells are produced.
      ii. active   passive   passive   passive   active

Unit 10.8

1. a. From left to right: lymphocyte; pathogen; antibody; antigen
   b. The antibodies may penetrate the pathogen and allow it to burst as water enters/phagocytes can be alerted by the presence of the antibody, and can then engulf and digest the pathogen
   c. vaccination

Unit 10.9

1. a. i. colon
      ii. rectum
      iii. small extension of caecum on LH side of diagram
   b. i. cholera
      ii. diarrhoea – colon is unable to reabsorb water due to a salt imbalance
   c. The pathogen (bacterium) is transmitted in faeces/clean water is treated to kill bacteria

Unit 11.1

1. a. M: trachea N; bronchus O; bronchiole
   b. Label lines to intercostal (between the rib) muscles and the diaphragm (below lungs)
   c. growth/cell division/active transport/heat generation
   d. carbon dioxide/water vapour

Unit 11.2

1. a. Oxygen from alveolus to blood, and carbon dioxide from blood to alveolus.

   b. large surface area/moist lining/very thin walls/closeness to capillary system
   c. pulmonary artery
2. a. emphysema or COPD
   b. Reduction of surface area available for gas exchange as walls of air sacs are destroyed.
3. glucose + oxygen   carbon dioxide + water + energy

Unit 11.3

1. a. lung
   b. Label a line drawn across the thorax below the lung.
   c. external intercostal muscles
   d. Intercostal muscles relax so front of thorax falls. Diaphragm relaxes so bottom of the thorax rises. Lung volume falls, so air is pushed out (exhaled).

Unit 12.1
Across
5. adenosine
6. heat
7. growth
9. active transport
10. respiration
12. mitochondria
13. oxidation
14. cell division
15. movement
16. triphosphate
18. glucose
19. protein
20. anaerobic
22. aerobic
23. light
24. liver

Down
1. solar
2. contraction
3. energy
4. photosynthesis
8. work
11. kilojoule
17. synthesis
21. oxygen

Unit 12.2

1. a. i. aerobic respiration
      ii. Towards the glass tube with the fruits in it.
      iii. The fruits use up oxygen, and the carbon dioxide they release is absorbed by the soda lime. Therefore the volume of gas inside the tube falls.
      iv. $\frac{40}{5} = 8$; $8 \times 0.25 = 2$ cm.
      Therefore the marker drop will be at 3.25 on the scale (i.e. current position is 5.25).
      v. Suitable control would be the tube as set up exactly the same but without the tomato fruits.
   b. Nitrogen gas does not allow respiration so that the fruits will not over-ripen and become 'spoiled'.

Unit 12.3

1. a. i. $C_6H_{12}O_6 + 6O_2 \rightarrow 6CO_2 + 6H_0 + $ energy
      ii. Respiration is catalysed by enzymes, which are affected by temperature.
   b. i. Pie chart B – most of the energy must be supplied by aerobic respiration as the athlete could not continue to run if anaerobic respiration was the energy supplier (much less efficient, and lactate is toxic).

ii. Performance is reduced as the lactic acid stops impulses reaching the muscle cells.

iii. The lactic acid is removed by diffusing into the blood.

c. The extra oxygen required to remove lactic acid accumulated during anaerobic exercise.

Unit 12.4

1. a. 7.6
   b. breathlessness/weakness/lightheadedness
   c. produce more red blood cells so can transport more oxygen
   d. more red blood cells makes blood thicker/more viscous so more likely to block coronary arteries
   e. testosterone/anabolic steroid increase muscle size/endurance

Unit 12.5

1. a. independent – type of fruit; dependent – rate of respiration; fixed – temperature/mass of fruit/volume of air available
   b. Type of fruit; Experiment 1; Experiment 2; Experiment 3; Mean rate of respiration of fruit (mm^3 used per min per g of fruit).
   c. Type of fruit on x axis, rate of respiration on y axis, bar chart, points plotted correctly.

Unit 13.1

1. a. The removal of toxins, the waste products of metabolism and substances in excess of requirements
   b. From top, and reading right to left: living cells; respiration; lungs; urea; liver; kidneys; absorption in gut; kidneys
   c. i. deamination (production of urea from excess amino acids)/storage of glycogen/removal of toxins such as alcohol
      ii. A – bile duct – bile; B – pancreatic duct – enzymes including amylase and protease; C – small intestine – food; D – hepatic portal vein – dissolved foods; E – hepatic artery – oxygenated blood; F – hepatic vein – deoxygenated blood

Unit 13.2

1. a. renal artery
   b. glomerulus
   c. The membrane is selective – pores are too small to allow passage of blood cells
   d. Mitochondria to supply energy for active transport/microvilli to provide increased surface area for absorption
   e. ureter

Unit 13.3

1. a. ammonia
   b. Optimum temperature for the enzyme urease.
   c. i. protein and glucose
      ii. They are reabsorbed in the kidney tubule.
   d. It is a control – to show that distilled water does not affect the biuret or Benedict's reagents.

Unit 14.1

1. a. A: sensory neurone; B: hair shaft
   b. i. It is raised.
      ii. Keeps a layer of air close to the skin, acting as a thermal insulator.
      iii capillary constricted, position the same
   c. This is a control system in which a deviation from the norm sets up a series of changes which cancel out the deviation.

Unit 14.2

1. a. line graph
   b. time taken to digest carbohydrates/absorb glucose
   c. i. insulin is secreted which increases uptake (and storage as glycogen) by liver and muscle
      ii. in negative feedback a change (rise in blood glucose) causes a process which reduces the effects of the change (release of insulin)

d. line graph
e. i. adrenaline is released/increases conversion of glycogen to glucose
   ii. increased heart rate/redistribution of blood from skin to muscles/pupils dilate/breathing rate increases/shallow depth of breathing

Unit 14.3

1. From the top of the table: A; C; E/F; E; D; B

Unit 14.4

1. a. i. nose
      ii. They always have a survival value, e.g. blinking clears the eye of particles of dust.
      iii. rapid/involuntary/short-lived/always have survival value
   b. i. 1 – receptor   2 – sensory neurone   3 – white matter   4 – grey matter   5 – association neurone   6 – synapse   7 – motor neurone
      ii. muscles – contract; glands – secrete (e.g. a hormone)

Unit 14.5

1. A
2. a. eye – to sight the ball; B nose – to smell; C touch receptor in skin – to feel the racquet in his hand; D semicircular canals in ear – detects position
   b. An electrical impulse, which travels as a wave of ion movements along the sensory neurones

Unit 14.6

1. a. From the top of the table: C; F; B; A; E; D
   b. i. stimulus is bright light; receptor is retina; co-ordinator is central nervous system; effector is iris; response is reduce diameter of pupil
      ii. Prevents bright light from damaging the retina.

Unit 14.7

1. a. Hormone: a chemical, produced by an endocrine organ, released into the bloodstream where it brings about a response at a target organ.
   Target organ: an organ which brings about a response to stimulation by a specific hormone.
   b. Hormones: slower/longer-lasting/more general than nervous control
2. a. Adrenaline is released – this stimulates the conversion of stored glycogen into soluble glucose.
   b. 1. Glucose must be absorbed from the gut – this takes a finite amount of time.
      2. Pupils dilate/skin becomes pale/hair stands on end/heart beats more quickly.

Unit 14.8

1. a. i. Auxin has moved downwards and to the non-illuminated side of the shoot.
      ii. Auxin moves to non-illuminated side – causes enlargement of cells on this side – shoot therefore bends towards the light.
      iii. response – (positive) phototropism; benefit – moves leaves into the optimum position for photosynthesis
   b. Co-ordinating formation of fruit for easier harvesting/acting as a weedkiller in growing crops

Unit 15.1

1. C
2. a. bar chart
   b. i. gonorrhoea
      ii. $\frac{4}{200} \times 100 = 2\%$
   c. Antibiotics are not effective against viral diseases
      Presence of antibiotics may select antibiotic-resistant bacteria

Unit 15.2

1. a. i. Effect of age on the likelihood of COPD
      ii. Chronic obstructive pulmonary disorder
      iii. No – there is no information about smoking, only about the age of sufferers from COPD.
   b. Vital capacity would fall. This is because smoking damages the alveoli so that they become less elastic. As a result they cannot stretch so the vital capacity is reduced.

Unit 15.3

1. If carbon monoxide combines with the haemoglobin, the red blood cells cannot carry so much oxygen. The developing fetus requires oxygen from its mother's blood, so will suffer if the mother has less oxygen in her red cells.
2. a. Smoker of 20 cigarettes per day has a risk factor of 2.3, a non-smoker has a risk factor of 0.1. Therefore a smoker is about 23 times more likely to die from lung cancer.
   b. Smoker of 1-14 cigarettes a day is 13 times more likely to die of lung cancer than a non-smoker.

Unit 16.1

1. a. i. asexual/binary fission (accept either)   ii. asexual
      iii. sexual   iv. sexual   v. sexual
   b. i. A clone is a group of identical cells produced by mitosis.
      ii. As all cells are identical they will be likely to be affected in the same way by any (possibly harmful) change.

Unit 16.2

1. a. mitosis in the second box in the asexual diagram, meiosis in the second box in the sexual diagram.
   b. for asexual   nn   and   nn; for sexual   n   and   n
   c. advantage: rapid/progeny well adapted to same environment as parents
      disadvantage: no variation possible, so great risk if 'unknown' infection attacks population
   d. Sexual reproduction would be used to provide a wide range of plants with different features.
      Any of the plants with desirable features, e.g. resistance to drought, could then be subjected to asexual reproduction, which would provide a large number of identical plants with the desirable feature.

Unit 16.3

1. a. Transfer of pollen from anther to the stigma.
   b. W: anther; X: ovary; Y: stigma; Z: petal
   c. Petals: small and dull-coloured; large and brightly coloured; attraction of insects
      Anthers: hang out into the wind; kept deep inside flower; anthers can release pollen into the wind
      Pollen: very light; heavy and produced in smaller quantities; light pollen can float in the wind
      Stigma: branched; deep within flower, strong; branched to catch wind-blown pollen/strong to avoid damage from visiting insect

Unit 16.5

1. a. i. Mark P on tip of stigma
      ii. stigma
   b. i. Show entry via the micropyle
      ii. Male nucleus fuses with female nucleus to form a diploid zygote. Permits variation by random combination of genetic material from parent plants.

Unit 16.6

1. a. From the top of the column: E; C; B; A; D; F
   b. Show pollen tube growth down style and entry to ovule via the micropyle
   c. i. plumule and radicle
      ii. starch
      iii. Iodine solution has changed from straw-brown to blue-black.

Unit 16.8

1. a. 2 – 10 – 22 – 15 – 1
   b. number of seeds in pod on x axis, number of pods on y axis, bars should be touching
   c. 6
   d. $\frac{22}{50} \times 100 = 44\%$

Unit 16.9

1. a. From left to right of bottom row: yes – no – yes – no – no – no
   b. Suitable temperature (for enzyme action)/water/presence of oxygen/unaffected by the presence or absence of light

Unit 16.10

1. a. A: sperm duct/vas deferens; B: urethra; C: testis; D: scrotal sac/scrotum; E: penis; F: prostate gland
   b. i.–v. in order; C; F; C; B; A
   c. E – A – D – B – F – C

Unit 16.11

1. a. They digest the coating of the female gamete to allow the head of the sperm to enter.
   b. Release energy by aerobic respiration – energy needed for beating of tail.
   c. 50 µm
   d. The sperm is haploid (just like the egg cell), and most body cells are diploid.
   e. Site: testis – ovary; Numbers: millions – few; Mobility: mobile – unable to move itself; Relative size: smaller – larger

Unit 16.12

1. a. i. pituitary gland
      ii. testosterone
   b. breasts – for production of milk; hips – to accommodate the growing fetus in the uterus
   c. menopause

Unit 16.13

1. a. i. 8
      ii. 2nd July
      iii. No egg cell is available.
   b. i. progesterone
      ii. oestrogen

Unit 16.14

1. a. From top of diagram: oviduct; ovary; uterus; vagina
   b. i. in oviduct
      ii. zygote
   c. From top of column: fertilisation; conception; copulation; AID; implantation; development

Unit 16.15

1. a. Prevents conception/prevents transmission of infected body fluids
   b. i. From the top of the column: 5 – 3 – 4 – 2 – 6 – 1
      ii. Combination of progesterone and oestrogen reduces the chance of ovulation (feedback inhibition). No ova available means no possibility of fertilisation/conception.
      iii. $1000 \times \frac{1}{20} = 50$.

Unit 16.16

1. a. i. amniotic cavity – contains amniotic fluid which acts as a shock absorber; uterus wall – muscular and so is protection against physical damage
      ii. from end of umbilical cord to wall of uterus
   b. glucose – from mother to fetus; haemoglobin – no movement across placenta; nicotine – from mother to fetus; amino acids – from mother to fetus; carbon dioxide – from fetus to mother; alcohol – from mother to fetus; urea – from fetus to mother

Unit 16.17
1. progesterone   falls   oxytocin   oestrogen   rises
2. a. i. gestation period
       ii. 38 weeks
   b. i. Head is the largest part so once it is out of the uterus the body can easily follow.
       ii. Contraction of the muscular walls of the uterus.

Unit 16.18
1. a. i. bacterium
       ii. painful urination
       iii. condom
   b. i. 2011
       ii. 2012
       iii. $\frac{18}{48.6} \times 100 = 39\%$
   c. i. Inhibits action of T-helper cells, so poor co-ordination of immune response.
       ii. AIDS is caused by a virus, so cannot be treated with an antibiotic.

Unit 17.1
1. a. i. gender at birth/eye colour/blood group
       ii. an alternative form of a gene
       iii. show a number of genes lined up along a thread-like chromosome
   b. i. 9
       ii. could be Rr or RR
       iii. $\frac{3}{4}$ or 75%

Unit 17.2
1. a. GCCTATG
   b. i. messenger RNA
       ii. ribosome
   c. amino acid
   d. i. protein
       ii. haemoglobin - antibodies - can recognise and bind to a neurotransmitter - enzyme which breaks down fats to fatty acids and glycerol - keratin

Unit 17.3
1. deoxyribonucleic acid; Watson; Crick; Franklin
2. From the top of the table: TRUE; FALSE; TRUE; TRUE; TRUE; TRUE; FALSE; TRUE; TRUE; TRUE
3. C

Unit 17.4
1. a. nucleus   b. white   c. B   d. identical twins
   e. i. identify which individuals are most closely related and do not let them breed with one another
       ii. examine DNA fingerprint and see how many different fingerprints (perhaps different species) there are in the new habitat
   f. i. C
       ii. 84

Unit 17.5
1. a. Male nerve cell: 46 XY; female white blood cell: 46 XX; sperm cell: 23 X or Y; egg cell: 23 X; red blood cell: 0 none
   b. mitosis
2. a. i. B
       ii. D
   b. bone marrow

Unit 17.6
1. a. One large and one small in each of the daughter cells
   b. i. ovary/testis
       ii. anther/ovule
   c. To reduce the number of chromosomes to half so that at fertilisation the 'normal' (diploid) number is restored

Unit 17.7
1. gene   meiosis   haploid   fertilisation   diploid
   recessive   heterozygous
2. genotype – the set of alleles present in an organism; homozygous – having two identical alleles; dominant – an allele that is always expressed if it is present; heterozygous – having two alternative alleles; recessive – allele that is only expressed in a homozygous individual; chromosome – a thread-like structure of DNA…; allele – one alternative form of a gene; phenotype – the observable features of an organism

Unit 17.8
1. a. i. Andrew and John
       ii. blood group – a discontinuous variation, so affected by genes only
       iii. nutrition – David might eat more high-calorie foods, or take less exercise
   b. codominance

Unit 17.9
1. a. Dominant: N; Recessive: n
   b. Philip: Nn; Janet: Nn
   c. i. nn
       ii. Nn or NN
   d. $\frac{1}{4}$ or 25%
   e. Pancreatic duct can be blocked by sticky mucus, so these enzymes cannot enter the duodenum and the foods are not digested.

Unit 17.10
1. a. 2 has two X chromosomes, 3 has two X chromosomes, 5 has one X and one Y chromosome
   b. 2 could have H and h, 3 could have h and h, 5 could be h
   c. female – female – female – male – male
   d. i. $X^h X^h$
       ii. Punnett square
       iii. 25%

Unit 18.1
1. continuous variation – a form of variation with many intermediate forms between the extremes; gene – a section of DNA responsible for an inherited characteristic; discontinuous variation – a form of variation with clear-cut differences between groups; phenotype – the observable features of an organism; height in humans – one example of continuous variation; environment – this factor, in addition to genotype, can affect phenotype; nutrients – one possible form of environmental influence on variation; blood group – one example of discontinuous variation.
2. a. i. Organisms with so many common features that they may interbreed and produce fertile offspring.
       ii. A change in the type or quantity of DNA in an individual.
       iii. A section of DNA responsible for coding for a single protein/characteristic.
   b. radiation/carcinogenic chemicals such as tar in cigarette smoke

Unit 18.2
1. a. artificial – artificial – natural – natural – natural
   b. i. By selecting individual animals with a high milk yield, breeding them, then selecting from their offspring cows that have a high milk yield, then breeding them, and so on.
       ii. resistance to disease/ability to withstand difficult environmental conditions such as low temperatures

Unit 18.3
1. a. B - E - C - A - D
   b. Heron – feeds by spearing fish and frogs; hawk – captures Florida rabbits and other mammals; spoonbill – filters algae and other small organisms from the water; finch – feeds on nuts and other hard fruits; warbler – feeds by catching small insects

Unit 18.4
1. **a.** Brussels sprouts – bud; broccoli – flower
   b. **i.** They have been produced by mitosis, so there is very little possibility of genetic variation.
   ii. nitrate – the ion needed for protein synthesis (growth); plants in closed environment – temperature and humidity can be controlled so that cuttings do not dry out

Unit 18.5
1. **a.** $1 - 2 - 4 - 6 - 10 - 5 - 3 - 2 - 1$
   b. mass category on x axis, number in group on y axis, bars should be touching
   c. Continuous variation
   d. A result of a combination of genotype and effects of the environment.

Unit 19.1
1. **a.** $0.5 \times 0.5 = 0.25 \text{ m}^2$
   b. There is a total of 60 springtails in 25 quadrats = 2.4 springtails per 0.25 m^2. Therefore there is a mean number of $2.4 \times 4 = 9.6$ springtails per m^2.
   c. They will not dry out/hidden from predators/can find rotting vegetation for food

Unit 19.2
1. food chain – the transfer of energy from one organism to the next, beginning with a producer; food web – a network of interconnected food chains; producer – an organism that makes its own organic nutrients, usually through photosynthesis; consumer – an organism that gets its energy by feeding on other organisms; herbivore – an animal that gets its energy from eating plants; carnivore – an animal that gets its energy by eating other animals; decomposer – an organism that gets its energy from dead or waste material
2. Pyramid should have broad base, of algae, then gradually narrowing through water fleas, smelt, and to the pointed peak at kingfisher.

Unit 19.3
1. **a.** algae - water flea - diving beetle - trout - kingfisher
   b. smelt/trout/diving beetle
   c. pyramid of numbers

Unit 19.4
1. **a.** **i.** the Sun
   ii. feeding
   iii. some is reflected/the wrong wavelength/does not fall on leaves
   iv. respiration – energy is lost here as heat
   b. **i.** A: $\frac{15000}{90000} \times \frac{100}{1} = 16.6\%$; B: $\frac{2000}{15000} \times \frac{100}{1} = 13.3\%$
   ii. Each stage in the food chain allows a loss of energy as heat. Fewer steps, as in eating a vegetarian diet, mean that more energy is transferred as this heat loss.

Unit 19.5
1. **a.** **i.** C: 28; D: 17
   ii. For C (greatest loss in mass), the environment is moist to provide water and large holes in mesh bag allow entry of oxygen.
   iii. C has larger holes so more oxygen can diffuse into the bag.
   iv. So that the bags themselves did not decompose.
   b. fungi and bacteria

Unit 19.6
1. **a.** From left to right: photosynthesis; respiration; feeding; decay
   b. It would raise the carbon dioxide concentration in the air.

Unit 19.7
1. **a.** **i.** B – feeding; E – denitrification
   ii. decomposition/decay by bacteria and fungi
   b. **i.** ammonium concentration would rise/nitrite and nitrate levels would fall/fewer dead leaves would be decomposed
   ii. ticks in few scavenging insects/regular turning of the heap to add air

Unit 19.8
1. **a.** higher death rate/less food/lower birth rate/emigration
   b. vaccination/immunisation programmes; use of antibiotics; improved surgical techniques; fewer deaths at childbirth
   c. use of antibiotics/antiseptics; thorough cooking to reduce food-poisoning bacteria

Unit 19.9
1. **a.** time on x axis, number of bacteria on y axis
   b. sugar – energy from respiration; amino acids – protein synthesis; sterile – prevent competition from other bacterial species
   c. show steepest part of curve
   d. shortage of oxygen/nutrients, e.g. glucose or amino acids

Unit 20.1
1. **a.** gene – a section of DNA coding for a protein; plasmid – a small circle of DNA in a bacterial cell; vector – a structure which can carry a gene into another cell; ligase – an enzyme that can splice one gene into another section of DNA; restriction – an enzyme that can cut a specific gene from a chromosome; sticky ends – pieces of single-stranded DNA left exposed after a gene is cut from a chromosome; fermenter – a vessel in which engineered bacteria can produce a valuable product under optimum conditions
   b. insulin – control of blood sugar level; factor 8 – one step in blood clotting; pectinase – 'clears' fruit juices by breaking up clumps of plant tissue; human growth hormone – can increase growth rate in humans of short stature
   c. the virus might not be completely inactivated, and thus may infect a patient with hepatitis

Unit 20.2
1. **a.** $100 - 3 = 97\%$
   b. each stage in the food chain allows a loss of energy as heat. Fewer steps, as in eating a vegetarian diet, mean that more energy is transferred with this heat loss.
   c. Insecticides may be present in the bodies of insects eaten by birds. The birds then accumulate the insecticide by eating many insects – this may harm the birds, e.g. affect egg laying.
   d. Identify gene offering resistance; introduce gene to bacterium via plasmid; infect plant with bacterium; select seedlings resistant to pesticide.

Unit 20.3
1. loss of habitat for animals/possible soil erosion/changes to water cycle/possible loss of valuable medicinal plants
2. **a.** **i.** Marsh has been drained/hedges have been removed/there are more buildings in 2003.
   ii. Marsh animals would be reduced in number, e.g. frogs need water in which to lay their eggs; hedge removal would mean fewer nesting sites for birds; hedge removal would eliminate certain food plants for insects such as butterflies.
   b. Loss of nesting sites/soil erosion/loss of food plants for some species/less removal of carbon dioxide from the atmosphere/disturbance of water cycle.

Unit 20.4
1. **a.** **i.** beans
   ii. rice
   iii. vitamins and minerals
   b. drought/loss of nutrients from soil/displacement of populations by war

Unit 20.5
1. **a.** The gases form a layer around the Earth which allows radiation in but does not allow thermal radiation out – the surface of the Earth therefore becomes warmer.
   b. **i.** These renewable energy resources do not produce greenhouse gases.
   ii. Insulation means less heat loss so less combustion of fossil fuels for heating.
   iii. Reforestation increases the number of plants which can remove carbon dioxide from the atmosphere during photosynthesis.

2. Removal of habitat for road construction/disturbance of wildlife by noise and presence of humans/pollution from vehicle exhausts

Unit 20.6
1. a. C–E–B–D–A
   b. Run-off of fertilisers from nearby farmland.
   c. Bacteria respire aerobically, using dead plants as food source. Aerobic respiration by bacteria reduces oxygen concentration in the water.
      Fish and larger invertebrates die as they are short of oxygen.

Unit 20.7
1. Management of the environment to maintain biodiversity.
2. a. i. Environmental factor: removal of bamboo forests – bamboo shoots are the basic food of the Giant Panda
      Biological factor: pandas reproduce very slowly – number of births does not replace number of dying pandas, so population falls
   ii. Saving the panda (a very attractive species which many people will help to conserve) also protects other species in the same habitat.
   b. i. To find the population size at the start of the management plan.
   ii. Many examples possible, e.g. butterflies – with nets, beetles – with pitfall traps, plants – with quadrats.

Unit 20.8
1. More shoals of fish are located, and more are caught by the fine mesh. Few fish escape to breed, so the population decreases. Loss of one species will affect the numbers of other species in the food web for this habitat.
2. Increase size of mesh/restrict areas in which fishing can take place/restrict times of year in which fishing can take place/limit the size of the catch for each fishing vessel.

Unit 20.9
1. a. A process which does not affect the environment for future generations.
   b. Less competition for light/for nutrients/for water.
   c. Limited food variety for animals/any pest or disease can affect all of the plants.
   d. Any will be a benefit. Best might be fast growth (so product is available quickly), resistance to disease (so few plants are lost to disease) and good growth on poor soil (so few fertilisers are necessary).

Unit 20.10
1. a. carbon dioxide + water $\rightarrow$ glucose + oxygen
      this process is driven by light energy
   b. The biocoil must be transparent to allow light to penetrate to the algae.
   c. The algae are removed to use as a fuel – they must be replaced quickly if the process is to be economical.

Unit 20.11
1. a. i. photosynthesis
      ii. diffusion
      iii. it is raised
   b. i. They are easier to decompose/they are unlikely to harm wildlife which might consume them.
      ii. printing newspapers/as packaging/as toilet paper/as paper towels

Unit 21.1
1. a. From the top of the table: F; F; T; T; F; T; T; T; T; T; T; F
   b. Typical bacterium is one millionth of a metre wide/bacteria are larger than viruses/many bacteria are not harmful, they are useful/bacteria do not have a nucleus – they have 'naked' DNA

Units 21.2
1. a. Sugar is the raw material for respiration, which provides the energy for bacterial multiplication.
   b. To maintain the optimum temperature for the activity of bacterial enzymes, and to avoid damage to protein products.

c. (6–)7 days: this represents the maximum yield of penicillin – any time longer produces less penicillin and would be expensive in terms of energy and raw materials.
d. Some bacteria in the population have a natural resistance – the non-resistant bacteria are killed by the antibiotic – the resistant bacteria now multiply and produce a resistant population.
e. Pectinase; protease; removes milk sugar from milk

Unit 21.3
1. a. i. To carry out respiration and release carbon dioxide. If water was substituted for sugar, no respiration could occur.
      ii. independent – type of sugar; dependent – volume of carbon dioxide produced
      iii. So that an accurate measurement of carbon dioxide volume could be made.
      iv. The concentration of sugar has fallen – it has become the limiting factor.
   b. glucose $\rightarrow$ ethanol + carbon dioxide
   c. Increase the temperature/increase the concentration of sugar/use purified enzymes from yeast

Unit 21.4
1. a. from the top: milk containing lactose; lactase; lactose-free milk
   b. Immobilisation – fixed onto an inert substance
      Importance – allows re-use of enzyme/provides product free of enzyme

Unit 21.5
a. $\frac{1000}{40} = 25$
   $25 \times 100 = 2500 \text{ cm}^3$
b. i. Pectinase is specific to breakdown of pectin. Amylase is a starch-digesting enzyme.
   ii. The higher temperature has increased enzyme activity, so more clear extract produced.

Exam-style questions
Unit 23
1. C
2. B
3. D
4. A
5. A
6. C
7. A
8. A
9. A
10. i. A ii. B iii. D
11. a. Correct position above and to the left of the stomach
    b. peristalsis
    c. From the top of the column: A – A – C – E – F
12. a. i. A: respiration; B: photosynthesis C: feeding D: respiration.
       ii. Decay/decomposition – a process in which organisms secrete enzymes which break down complex organic compounds such as proteins into simpler compounds such as amino acids/ammonium nitrate.
    b. i. In the compost heap respiration is taking place. This releases energy, some of which is lost as heat.
       ii. This allows oxygen to penetrate the compost – oxygen is needed for aerobic respiration.
13. a. i. large surface area/close to blood supply/moist lining
       ii. Allows stretching during the inhalation/exhalation cycle.
    b. Blood at A has more carbon dioxide and less oxygen than blood at B.
    c. Makes lung tissue less elastic/breaks down walls of alveoli/inactivates cilia in airways/may trigger development of cancer cells.
14. a. A - 3;   B - 4;   C - 2;   D - 1
    b. i. meiosis   ii. mitosis
    c. i. stem cell   ii. bone marrow
15. a. G = Pp   K = PP
    b. two (D and E)

    c. 0 (0%)

    d. 0.5 (50%)

16. a. Temperature affects the activity of the enzymes which catalyse respiration, so experiment B will have enzymes working less efficiently.

    b. i. To prevent diffusion of oxygen from the air (keep respiration anaerobic).

        ii. Boiling removes oxygen from the solution.

    c. $C_6H_{12}O_6 \rightarrow 2C_2H_5OH + 2CO_2$

17. a. i. apple tree - apple moth caterpillar - thrush - owl

        ii. sunlight

    b. i. pyramid of biomass

        ii. the position of an organism in a food chain

        iii. Energy is lost (respiration) at each trophic level so that less than 100% is transferred from one trophic level to the next. As much as 90% is lost at each transfer, so there can be very few transfers.

        iv. loss of habitat/breeding site; hunting; loss of food source/prey captive breeding; provision of nature reserve; ban on hunting

18. a. raises blood pressure (which can damage narrow capillaries)

    b. i. 0.2 – 2.5 g

        ii. (0.2 + 0.9 + 2.0 + 2.5 + 0.7 + 0.5 + 1.3) = 8.1

           8.1 – 6.0 = 2.1 g

    c. toast and butter (butter is derived from milk)

You will find that the practical paper or the alternative to practical will be much more straightforward if you recognise certain standard pieces of equipment, and understand what they are used for.

Apparatus and materials

Safety equipment appropriate to the work being planned, but at least including eye protection such as safety spectacles or goggles.

3D image	Name and function	Diagram
	■ **Watch glass**: used for collection and evaporating liquids with no heat, and for immersing biological specimens in a liquid.	
	■ **Filter funnel**: used to separate solids from liquids, using a filter paper.	
	■ **Measuring cylinder**: used for measuring the volume of liquids.	
	■ **Thermometer**: used to measure temperature.	

The other very important measuring device in the laboratory is a balance (weighing machine).

	■ **Spatula**: used for handling solid chemicals; for example, when adding a solid to a liquid.	
	■ **Pipette**: used to measure and transfer small volumes of liquids.	
	■ **Stand, boss, and clamp**: used to support the apparatus in place. This reduces the risk of dangerous spills. This is not generally drawn. If the clamp is merely to support a piece of apparatus, it is usually represented by two crosses as shown.	
	■ **Bunsen burner**: used to heat the contents of other apparatus (e.g. a liquid in a test tube) or for **directly heating solids**.	HEAT
	■ **Tripod**: used to support apparatus above a Bunsen burner. **The Bunsen burner, tripod, and gauze are the most common way of heating materials in school science laboratories.**	
	■ **Gauze**: used to spread out the heat from a Bunsen burner and to support the apparatus on a tripod.	
	■ **Test tube and boiling tube**: used for heating solids and liquids. They are also used to hold chemicals while other substances are added and mixed. They need to be put safely in a test tube rack.	
	■ **Evaporating dish**: used to collect and evaporate liquids with or without heating.	
	■ **Beaker**: used for mixing solutions and for heating liquids.	

Table of hazard symbols

Symbol	Description	Examples	Symbol	Description	Examples
	Oxidising These substances provide oxygen which allows other materials to burn more fiercely.	Bleach, sodium chlorate, potassium nitrate		**Harmful** These substances are similar to toxic substances but less dangerous.	Dilute acids and alkalis
	Highly flammable These substances easily catch fire.	Ethanol, petrol, acetone		**Corrosive** These substances attack and destroy living tissues, including eyes and skin.	Concentrated acids and akalis
	Toxic These substances can cause death. They may have their effects when swallowed or breathed in or absorbed through the skin.	Mercury, copper sulfate		**Irritant** These substances are not corrosive but can cause reddening or blistering of the skin.	Ammonia, dilute acids and alkalis

Reagent	Use in biology
hydrogencarbonate indicator (bicarbonate indicator)	Detects changes in carbon dioxide concentration, for example in exhaled air following respiration
✖ iodine in potassium iodide solution (iodine solution)	Detection of starch
✖ Benedict's solution (or an alternative such as Fehling's)	Detection of a reducing sugar, such as glucose
⬛ biuret reagent(s) (sodium or potassium hydroxide solution and copper sulfate solution)	Detection of protein
⬛ ethanol/methylated spirit	For dissolving lipids in testing for the presence of lipids. Also used to remove chlorophyll from leaves during starch testing.
cobalt chloride paper	Detects changes in water content
pH indicator paper or Universal Indicator solution or pH probes	Detects changes in pH during reactions such as digestion of fats to fatty acids and glycerol
litmus paper	Qualitative detection of pH
glucose	Change in water potential of solutions
sodium chloride	Change in water potential of solutions
aluminium foil or black paper	Foil can be used as a heat reflector: black paper as a light absorber
a source of distilled or deionised water	Change in water potential of solutions. Also used in making up mineral nutrient solutions.
eosin/red ink	To follow the pathway of water absorbed by plants
limewater	A liquid absorbent for carbon dioxide, for example in exhaled air
✖ methylene blue	A stain for animal cells
⬛ potassium hydroxide	Removes carbon dioxide from the atmosphere, for example during experiments on conditions for photosythesis
sodium hydrogencarbonate (sodium bicarbonate)	Very mild alkali: used for adjusting pH of solutions for enzyme activity
vaseline/petroleum jelly (or similar)	Blocks pores such as stomata, and so prevents water loss